LEADING FOR ENGAGEMENT

7 SINS AND 7 SECRETS

First published in 2022

ISBN: 978-1-86922-940-5 (Printed)
eISBN: 978-1-86922-941-2 (PDF Ebook)

Published by KR Publishing
P O Box 3954
Randburg
2125
Republic of South Africa

Tel: (011) 706-6009
E-mail: orders@knowres.co.za
Website: www.kr.co.za

Printed and bound: HartWood Digital Printing, 243 Alexandra Avenue, Halfway House, Midrand
Typesetting, layout and design: Parsley Studios, info@parsley.co.za
Cover design: Marlene De Lorme, marlene@knowres.co.za and Parsley Studios
Editing and Proofreading: Mandy Collins, mcollins@icon.co.za

Project management: Cia Joubert, cia@knowres.co.za

LEADING FOR ENGAGEMENT

7 SINS AND 7 SECRETS

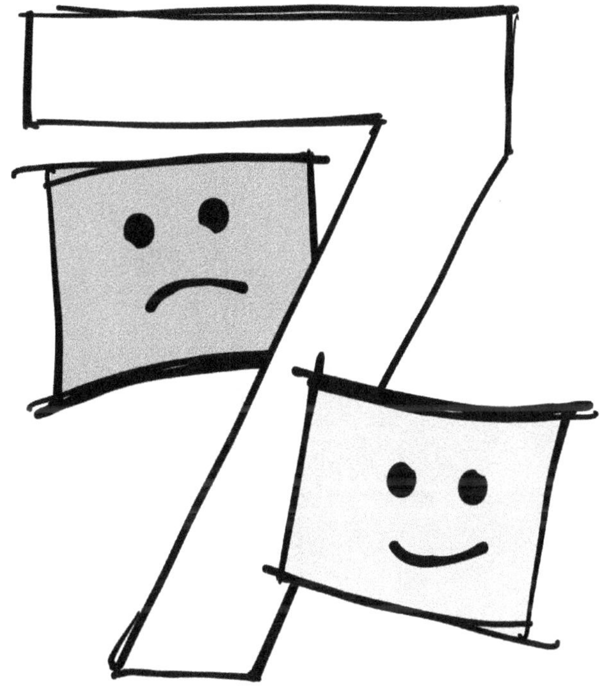

Tracey Swanepoel

kr

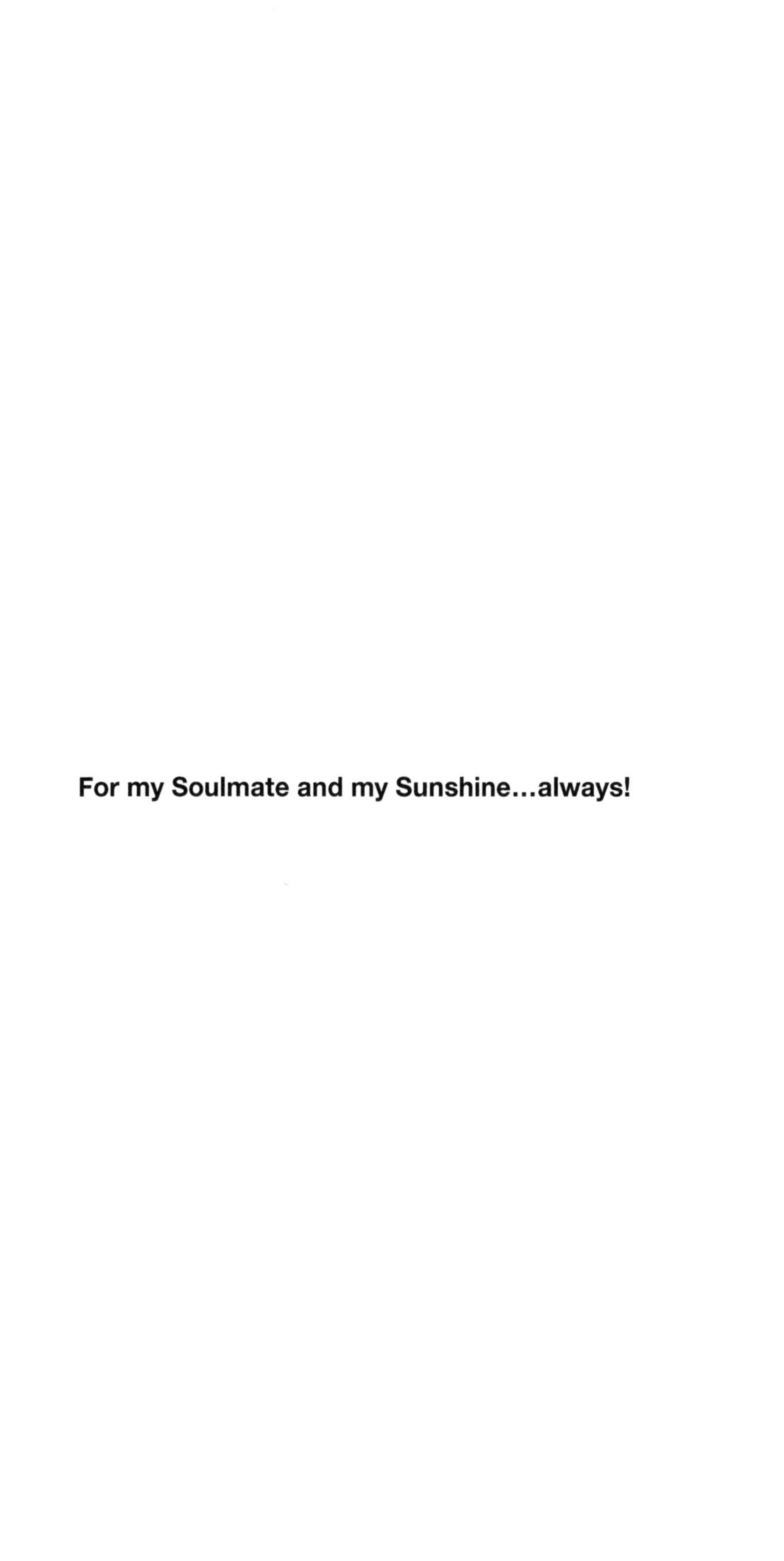

For my Soulmate and my Sunshine…always!

ENDORSEMENTS

All over the world the performance of organisations is suffering because of the so-called Employee Disengagement Plague, induced by poor leadership. Regrettably South Africa is no exception. Tracey Swanepoel provides a fully integrated solution in a very practical, thoughtful way. Her case studies illustrating "sins" and "secrets" make compelling reading and are easy to convert into personal action plans. More importantly, her passion for people and their morale, motivation and fulfillment shines through and inspires. This book is compulsory reading for leaders who want to turbocharge their effectiveness and the significance of their legacy, for the good of all.

Brand Pretorius
Retired Chief Executive of McCarthy Limited

It is an understatement to say that today the world needs better, more engaged, empathetic, and authentic leaders that truly care about their people. Thank you to an outstanding author, Tracey Swanepoel, for nailing the essence of leadership with extraordinarily useful insights and for sharing her own bold and vulnerable leadership journey, and key lessons learnt. This takes character and courage.

This book is filled with robust, practical tips and tools of desired leadership models - showing what we should be aspiring to in these challenging times.

The content is compelling and poignant for both current and aspiring leaders. Read it!

Dr Shirley Zinn
Chair and Independent Non-Executive Director of Boards

This is a book about leading to engage - through better communication, more understanding of what's really happening and connecting people to purpose. When leaders ask me about building staff engagement, I often tell them the best way to build engagement is to stop doing things that piss staff off. Whilst I firmly believe this is true, it falls into the category of 'interesting, but not useful'. Fortunately, there are thinkers like Tracey Swanepoel who can unpack the 'power skill' of staff engagement and provide a practical and useful guide to help leaders be their best - to create a workplace that energises and empowers staff and to lead their organisation to success. This book will help transform the way you think about leadership.

Mark Schenk, Managing Director, Anecdote International

This is a must-read book for all leaders who are committed to create organisations where people are inspired to make their best contribution. This book describes a future that many of us are committed to… with clear guidance on how to get there. My hope is that leaders will apply what they have learnt from reading this book to lead courageously and authentically in order to turn their organisations into communities of belonging and contribution.

Dr Louise van Rhyn – Founder of Symphonia and Designer of Partners for Possibility and Convener, Africa Leadership Week

---

Tracey's latest contribution reminded me that like investing, leadership isn't rocket science - you must just get the basics right. That applies equally to the art and science of leadership, the focus of this book. Most readers will have come across Tracey's seven sins and seven secrets in different forms, but the strength of this concise volume is that the logic of these leadership principles is supported by practical examples encouraging liberal use of them. The results from such application are sure to surprise – on the upside!

Alec Hogg, Founder, BizNews

This book is not only well and practically written but absolutely aligns with my findings, realisations and potential solutions after 20+ years in the leadership space. Please read it. You won't regret one moment of doing so. One senses Tracey's years of experience through her own eyes and others close to her. A really great book.

Adriaan Groenewald
Leadership Activist and Co-Founder ThinkLead Ecosystem

Tracey's simple but insightful approach to flush out the potential stumbling blocks to leaders and companies reaching their full potential (greatness) is a must read for all leaders who want to make a difference. At some point, most of us as leaders come to the realisation that your best leadership tool is your authentic self. Finding the confidence to do so is a journey and this amazing book can be a useful and practical guide along the way.

Nolitha Fakude, Chairperson, Anglo American South Africa and President, Minerals Council South Africa

---

TABLE OF CONTENTS

ABOUT THE AUTHOR

Tracey Swanepoel completed her BA Communication (Hons) at RAU (cum laude) and her MBA at Henley Business School. She has a deep understanding of strategy, leadership, culture and change management and has pioneered a unique methodology which equips leaders with practical tools to engage employees and enhance business's performance. She started her career in advertising, working as a strategic planner for FCB, Ogilvy and Grey Worldwide. After completing her MBA dissertation she spent five years at Harmony Gold as internal strategy executive before starting her own consulting business, THINKspiration in 2008. Tracey speaks and writes extensively on strategy, culture and leadership issues facing business and is passionate about developing practical solutions. Tracey's first book, *The Leadership Riptide and How to Escape* was published in 2016, and was selected by the SABPP (South African Board of People Practices) in 2017 as one of their top 5 leadership books.

FOREWORD

If I had the talent to write, this is the book I would have wanted to write!

Not only does it capture in beautiful and simple language what I truly believe, but it also shares wisdom and practical tips from a real subject matter expert, who is bold and vulnerable enough to share her own leadership and engagement journey with us as her readers. This is an amazing book by an amazing person on her journey, a journey which I have had the privilege of sharing for the past twenty-one years.

Nobody ever asks (or allows) their husbands or life partners to write the foreword to their book on 'leadership for engagement'! Ja sure!

I happen to have been happily married to Tracey for the past eighteen years, but that is almost beside the point. I am indeed her biggest fan, her most longstanding professional client and for the last decade her colleague (employee, if truth be told!).

So, the story of this book and Tracey's own leadership journey predates that fateful day in late March 2000 when our paths crossed for the first time in a dilapidated meeting room at the Randfontein Estates Gold Mine Golf Club. Harmony, the gold mining company I had run as CEO for the previous five and a half years, had just concluded a successful surprise (unsolicited or some would say 'hostile') takeover of Randfontein Estates. Shareholders of both companies were ecstatic, Harmony's employees and unions were at best confused and Randfontein's employees from top to bottom were outright hostile. Not the ideal environment to implement the 'Harmony Way' or to set out to realise the value we believed we could create (some of which had already been paid out as a takeover premium) through the very people who called us the 'nazis in jeans' to our faces.

I asked the company Tracey was consulting to at the time for help with how to close the gap between external stakeholders (who were excited about the company's strategy) and the most important stakeholders, our employees, who were not excited at all. As I said, at best they were confused, at worst they were outright negative or even hostile!

What started as an intervention to address internal marketing/ communication became a journey of discovering how to get employees aligned to the corporate strategy to the point that they became truly excited to 'play' their part in delivering that strategy.

Some years later, after another audacious bid (again some would call it hostile) when Harmony tried to take over Goldfields (a company twice its size) the results of our 'intervention turned into a journey' at Harmony spoke volumes! After seven months of public hostilities which played out on the front pages of national and international newspapers, our bid failed. This time we couldn't convince external stakeholders (like the judges presiding over the numerous frivolous court challenges) yet most importantly, it was our employees who were as excited about our strategy as our shareholders (and Goldfields' shareholders for that matter!) were.

So, now you know I am a Tracey fan, and a believer in what she teaches and implements when she assists companies to do this! But what exactly is 'this'? In short, 'this' is what the book is about.

In its most beautiful simplicity, the role of a leader is to give hope by painting a compelling picture of an inspiring future. If as a leader you are not the top dog, defining this strategy (clear picture of the future) may not be your role, but you still need to help your team to be excited by it and to be aligned to it. It is this simple two-step process (i.e. defining a compelling future and aligning your team to it), rather than some complicated consultant-driven list of activities that results in engagement, the buzzword of the moment.

In her first book: *The Leadership Riptide and How to Escape*, Tracey makes a compelling case for the fact that although science clearly indicates what we should be doing as leaders, the reality is that in most instances, current 'best practice' seems to be almost the exact opposite! In this book she takes this further with specific reference to how our current leadership paradigm (and the so-called 'best practices') prevent us from achieving the nirvana of fully engaged employees, who are passionately pursuing the corporate strategy whilst fulfilling their individual purpose and having some fun in the process.

She identifies seven sins that plague current corporate leadership practices, but also then outlines seven simple and practical solutions, or in her language: secrets.

The second part of the book resonates so well with my own struggles and hopefully growth as a leader. If only I knew at the start of my career that leadership is both hard, but also easy. The hard part is to be brave enough to get to know yourself and then to be prepared to be the authentic you. The easier part is to learn to listen (after you have learned to shut up) and then to discover how to connect with people through the power of storytelling. I don't regret much of my journey as a leader, but I passionately work with Tracey in THINKpiration to help other (and especially younger) leaders to develop both these hard and easy skills.

I don't know how (or for that matter why) one would lead a team of people without the simple and practical process explained in part three. This, in my experience, works as well in the business world as it does in the NPO/NGO world. And although being an elected political leader is not on my radar, I really wish that some of them would read part three of this book!

For those who have read this far, but may not get to the crux of this book, let me give you the four steps to success if you need to lead others (which is discussed in part three):

1. Paint a compelling picture of the future.
2. Listen to your people in order to understand where they are.
3. Distil this into a compelling story and if possible, visualise it. (At THINKspiration, we actually call this a Visual Map)
4. Empower (coach and allow) all leaders/supervisors to use the map to create context for all the conversations that could possibly take place in your organisation or the part of it that you are leading.

This book lives up to its own clearly stated formula. It paints a very clear picture of the desired leadership model we should all aspire to. The intellectual case for why we need to change from the habits, practices and trappings of the current paradigm is made clearly and in a compelling way. That clear picture is exactly what gives us hope that there is indeed the possibility of a better world of work. And finally, Tracey shares some practical advice on how each one of us can achieve that, whilst still being authentic and true to ourselves.

Lastly, don't take my word for it. Read the damn book!

Bernard Swanepoel
February 2022

INTRODUCTION

At the age of 10, my big dream was to win Wimbledon. I never did (or you would have heard!). But I did spend the next 10 years of my life chasing a little green ball around the tennis court – ultimately ending up with a tennis scholarship at a US university.

Tennis taught me a lot about strategy and leadership: that you don't have to be bigger to be better (well, at five feet, two inches I had to believe this one), that you can outWIT rather than outHIT opponents, and that to chase a dream, you have to visualise it so clearly that you can make decisions today based on the future that you want to create.

Towards the end of my time as a player, when I made the seemingly natural transition to coaching, I experienced quite the revelation. We tend to think that if you play a sport well, then coaching is a doddle, something that comes naturally. Nothing could be further from the truth!

As a player you rely completely and utterly on your own technical skill set to get results. As a coach, it's a completely different ball game (no pun intended!): coaching is all about how you motivate, inspire, influence and lead others to access their own skills and perform at their best.

This is equally true in the corporate world. How often do we see the meteoric rise of technically skilled, star "performers/players"? Instead of being able to rely on their own (often exceptional) ability, they find themselves confronted by the reality that their success now depends on the performance of others.

How do their technical skills and unique abilities serve these leaders in their capacity of coach rather than star player? Not well! Because getting colleagues/teammates to perform at their peak requires different skills. Inevitably the stakes are high – it's all about results. Results comprise the collective effort of all the teams that make up the business: be it five, fifty, five hundred or fifty thousand people.

For many a leader, the realisation dawns that the skills that may have got you here, are not the skills that are going to "get you there"

For many a leader, the realisation dawns that the skills that may have got you here, are not the skills that are going to "get you there".

The right stuff?

With a match-winning performance in mind, where should you, as a leader, start? There may be existing practices and processes that make sense: a strategic planning session where you identify "big, hairy, audacious goals" and the plans to achieve these; teambuilding interventions to get your top team to gel; the business planning cycle that injects the certainty of forecasts and projections into an uncertain world.

Perhaps you have identified the need for a different, "better" culture – where employees feel empowered in their role, take responsibility and act as if this were their own business.

Possibly you are considering a more streamlined structure that you think would remove some bureaucracy and red tape, and would enable quicker, more efficient decisions and actions.

What about overhauling the reward and recognition system to incentivise the "right" behaviours and bolster performance?

This is not an exhaustive list. It's not even a bad list. All of the above are good things to do – even great things to do. But there's more... a whole lot more. Even the most amazing game plan and the most incredible coach can't win a match without the collective effort of the team on the field, who are playing in imperfect, real-life conditions, where neither the ball, the competitors, or the referee are perfectly predictable.

So the million dollar question is: how do you get the five or the five hundred or the five thousand or the fifty thousand people you lead to shoot the lights out?

An epic fail

Let me share what not to do: I was 27 when I was made the strategic director and head of department at one of South Africa's big advertising agencies. Thrilled and terrified, I was determined to make our team shine.

Thankfully, the team consisted of two junior planners and an intern. (I say "thankfully" because the damage I inflicted was limited to three people – and I'm deeply hopeful that it wasn't permanent).

With no appreciation that my job was now to get other people to perform, and no idea about leadership, I micro-managed these poor souls into the ground. Every idea they had, I overrode with my own spin on it; every slide they made, I changed. Pretty soon I was exhausted, burnt out – and my team were frustrated and demoralised.

Not one of us could care less about where the agency was going or what we could contribute to getting it there. We avoided those "strategic" presentations because we were far too busy with our own stuff. So we didn't add value to the agency, and we didn't shine.

It was only many years later that it hit me: because I behaved like a star player trying to win the match rather than a coach trying to get the best performance from my team, I committed an epic fail of leadership!

So now that it's clear what not to do: how should leaders/ coaches get results? As business we have put our faith in the "right stuff": strategy, business plans, performance management systems, communication, bonuses, incentives, rewards, to name a few. We believe that if we do the "right stuff", the people we lead will get the message, respond accordingly, and readily give body and soul to the cause.

Except that it simply isn't happening: it doesn't matter where you look in the world, employees are disengaged, and view work as a life sentence to be served, a means to an end. Some leaders may be aware of the disengagement plague – but perhaps haven't realised how directly it impacts on performance. Global research has proven repeatedly that even slightly disengaged employees will result in performance and productivity declines, cost overruns, and safety falling apart (Gallup meta-analysis).[1]

> Some leaders may be aware of the disengagement plague – but perhaps haven't realised how directly it impacts on performance.

What are we missing?

The link between a sustainable, high performing business and high levels of employee engagement is logical and proven. Yet, it's clear that engagement cannot happen in the absence of every leader actually connecting with his/her employees. Leaders need to stop treating engagement as something outside of them, something that can be outsourced. They need to stop hoping that somehow it will magically occur without them. Every leader needs to own the responsibility to "lead for engagement".

That's where the seven sins and seven secrets come in. If we look at most business's "fabric" (woven by the combination of their practices, procedures and culture) through an engagement lens, the seven sins that kill engagement are in plain sight. These are sins that have seeped into many corporate cultures and have become the "way we do things around here". They may not be deliberate, but that doesn't make them any less deadly.

However important it may be to illuminate what's wrong by identifying the seven sins and their seven commensurate secrets (part one of the book) – this is only a part of the solution. The bulk of this book (parts two and three) is about the seven secrets: each of which have been scientifically proven to foster engagement.

Knowing about the secrets is not enough, though – the big question is how can leaders put these secrets into practice? How can they make them happen?

you simply cannot lead others if you can't first lead yourself.

The answer comes in two parts: part two outlines a three-step plan for leaders in terms of leading themselves – because you simply cannot lead others if you can't first lead yourself.

Part three deals with leading others and takes the form of a four-step "leading for engagement" plan and process that has been tried, tested (and perfected) over the past twenty years.

Plans are all good and well. But ultimately this book is about you as a leader – standing on the edge of a rushing river. Across the river, on the other side you "see" the company you would love to create – the legacy that you would be proud to leave in your wake: an empowered workforce; a great place to work; employer of choice; best performer of the industry by all metrics.

The "business as usual" river rages and roils with undercurrents and challenges. Getting caught up in it means that your chances of reaching the other side are slim. You see seven stones indicating a route across. A plan. It's not easy, because you will have to go against the flow, deal with waves and tides and currents that will threaten to throw you off course. Do you cross? As you decide, remember where you have come from, and who you want to become! It's your choice!

PART ONE

Engagement: Seven Sins and Seven Secrets

Who is going to destroy me today?

Hardly a day goes by without yet another horror story from the world of work.

28 September 2016 was the day of my book launch for *The Leadership Riptide and How to Escape*. It was also my son Zack's class assembly, a big deal in Grade 5.

As I skidded in to one of the last remaining seats, I was pretty preoccupied with my thoughts about the launch, and so I was relieved to end up next to Lorna*, a mom I knew fairly well but who wasn't known for small talk. Nonetheless, as we sipped our coffee and waited for the proceedings to begin, I couldn't resist asking her about her new situation.

She had recently resigned from a big job in corporate finance (with its big title and big salary) to do her own thing. My first observation was that she looked 10 years younger: she was positively glowing! And as she talked about how well her new life was suiting her, she was exuberant.

"I love it. I'm discovering who I'm really meant to be," she bubbled. "But the best part by far is that I don't wake up every morning wondering who is going to destroy me today."

Then there's Sibongile*, a young, highly qualified and competent professional who works in one of the blue-chip corporates in the resources sector. Ambitious and passionate, she was really excited at being given the responsibility to initiate and drive a substantial and significant project from start to finish.

Imagine her disappointment, hurt and betrayal when she found out that her superiors had ripped away her passion project – without so much as informing her, leaving her to discover it herself when she wasn't included in a critical meeting.

Willem*, known for his brilliant functional skills, was an executive and one of the inner circle at a well-known South African corporate. Cue a leadership change, and suddenly Willem and a number of his colleagues were unceremoniously demoted, because the exco was too "large and unwieldy".

"I understand the need for it. But what I'm battling with is the sense of betrayal, the trust that has been broken. What is really in it for me to continue to give my heart and soul to this business?" he asked.

These experiences might sound "minor" in the greater scheme of things, but they leave us feeling exhausted, unappreciated, defeated. Large-scale tragedies like work-induced suicides, the daily trauma of trying to meet impossible targets, enduring the dreaded performance review, or merely surviving the day, result in our hearts racing, and fear flooding our veins – eventually coming to rest as a solid lump of dread in the pit of our stomachs. This, for most of us, is what it feels like to be at work.

The "Sunday scaries" are a thing

Maybe these stories trigger a litany of your own negative experiences. It's these negative experiences that distort our view of work, and its potential to give us meaning, purpose and a place to live out our potential.

It shouldn't have to be this way! As Studs Terkel puts it: "Work is about a search for daily meaning as well as daily bread, for recognition as well as cash, for astonishment, rather than torpor (lethargy); in short for a sort of life rather than a Monday through Friday sort of dying."[2]

And yet, right now, we dread Monday so much that there's a term for it: the Sunday scaries… which refer to that Sunday evening feeling of dread when it dawns on us that our freedom is over and its back to that "Monday through Friday sort of dying". A 2018 survey commissioned by LinkedIn found that 80% of working American adults worry about the upcoming work week on Sundays: hardly the picture of "tap dancing to work" that Warren Buffett often refers to.[3]

The engagement crisis: It's more than a feeling

These negative feelings and perceptions about work are corroborated by empirical evidence: Gallup's engagement statistics show that only 15% of employees worldwide are engaged, meaning that throughout the entire globe only 15% of employees are passionate, inspired and prepared to go the extra mile.[4]

The flipside of this indicates that 85% of employees are somewhere on the spectrum of disengagement: the least pernicious would be the so-called "dead wood" who keep their heads down, and watch the clock until "this too shall pass". At the far end of the disengagement continuum are the active saboteurs, who gleefully go out of their way to do their worst for the company.

A UK study found that one in two employees (50%) actually dread getting up to go to work in the morning, and that 59% have never had a happy moment at work. This adds further context to this sad picture.[5]

It's hardly surprising that the cost of mental health is soaring (it costs the UK economy an estimated £70 billion per annum in lost productivity and health care).[6] Work is literally killing our souls and sucking the life out of us.

Work is literally killing our souls and sucking the life out of us.

What does this mean for companies?

Where and how does all this unhappiness, stress and burnout among employees manifest? How does employee disengagement affect a business's productivity and performance?

Consider for a moment the issues that keep leaders awake at night and regularly dominate boardroom discussions: How do we deal with declining performance or ultimately non-performance? Why do we have continual over-expenditure? Why are we slacking off on our safety? Why are absenteeism and/or staff turnover out of control? How do we transform our toxic/fear-based culture into one that promotes diversity and inclusion and fosters innovation?

Leaders wear themselves out playing whack-a-mole with the "iceberg" problems – not realising that the real issue that can sink a business – disengagement – lies beneath its surface.

These are the issues leaders see clearly – the tip of the iceberg. Yet these issues (and many others) are linked by what lies beneath the surface – something that's impossible to spot unless you know it is there: engagement or the lack thereof. Engagement shows up in the attitude of employees, their discretionary effort, their passion, energy and problem-solving ability. Their initiative. Their willingness to go-the-extra-mile. Leaders wear themselves out playing whack-a-mole with the "iceberg" problems – not realising that the real issue that can sink a business – disengagement – lies beneath its surface.

What is engagement?

Despite our best efforts in terms of measurement and observation, we find engagement in a business difficult to define. But think for a moment of your favourite sports team, and more specifically of its fans. Whether it's cricket, rugby, football, baseball – the fans know the ins and outs of every move their team makes.

They know whether the coach has selected the right players, who's in form, out of form or injured, and who the best replacement is. Fans have opinions about what strategies the team should adopt to win their next match. And about the strategies that the opposition are likely to use. Fans don't receive incentives, recognition or payment of any description – they do what they do because of their love of their team and their love of the game. And their passion, knowledge, and expertise – their belonging (or what a business would term engagement) overflows.

Why should leaders and companies want it?

Imagine if we could create that same deep sense of belonging/engagement in the workplace. Imagine if instead of thinking of our employees as reluctant labourers, we thought of and treated them as fans.

Consider the impact on productivity – on performance – on the business as a whole? By not recognising engagement as a fundamental issue, we also miss the link between engagement, discretionary effort and value creation.

Let's say a company pays an employee R100. The company makes an automatic and unquestioned assumption that in return for that R100 it receives R100's worth of effort from the employee. So, pay R100 and get 100% return in effort. Right? Well, not quite.

Because what companies don't like to acknowledge is the uncomfortable truth that effort is given at the discretion of the employee/fan (i.e., discretionary effort). It's their choice.

If we use the Gallup engagement statistics (15% of employees are fully engaged) as an indication of discretionary effort, it means that for every R100 a company pays, it only gets 100% effort from 15% of its employees.[7] So the return on investment for 85% of its employees may range from less than 100% and perhaps even into the negative range. Who would invest in a share portfolio with these levels of return? Who wants to own or play for a team where only 15% of players are fully committed?

A shocking return on investment is one thing, but the more fundamental issue is the litany of problems that low engagement levels leave in their wake: the high absenteeism, dodgy safety performance, cost overruns, customer service issues, quality control lapses and many more. These are the problems that leaders need to face down and solve on a daily basis – and may sadly even exacerbate with short-term Band-Aids® (like bonuses and incentives) instead of addressing them systematically by improving engagement.

Engaged people are the secret to exceptional performance

So what's the link between running a successful, sustainable high performing business – leaving a leadership legacy to be proud of – and employee engagement? Most leaders, being technical experts, are trained to solve problems by applying their technical expertise.

But people are not problems to be solved. As one leader that that I worked with put it: "When I first started running this operation I thought it was all about the sums – if I could get the maths right, all my problems would be solved. Then when that didn't work, I thought it must be all about getting the technical solutions right… if I could get the engineering right, all my problems would be solved. Now I've realised that it's actually about the people, and doing everything I can as a leader to inspire them. I have finally realised that engaged people are the secret to exceptional performance."

People are not problems to be solved.

This is more than just intuitive wisdom: In 2020 Gallup consolidated four hundred and fifty-six research studies across two hundred and seventy-six organisations in fifty-four industries in ninety-six countries. Their objective was to investigate the relationship between employee engagement and performance outcomes.

In total, one hundred and twelve business units were studied, amounting to nearly three million employees. Eleven performance outcomes were studied, and employee engagement was found to be related to each of these.[8]

Across the companies, business units scoring in the top half on employee engagement more than doubled their odds of success as compared with the bottom half. Those in the ninety-ninth percentile had nearly five times the success rate of those at the first percentile. The differences between top quartile and bottom quartile engagement in companies accounted for:

- A 23% difference in terms of profitability
- A 64% difference in terms of safety incidents
- An 81% difference in terms of absenteeism

If leaders buy the argument that engagement makes business sense, then why are engagement scores at all-time lows? Why is the world of work overflowing with horror stories like those of Lorna, Sibongile and Willem where people/employees/fans are being broken down and sometimes destroyed? What practices are so inextricably part of the fabric of corporate life that they maintain the status quo? How can leaders change this?

To understand what to change, we need a fresh-eyed look at the world of work using the lens of engagement. Where do we go wrong and where could we go right?

Leading for engagement: Seven sins and seven secrets

The seven deadly sins are a classification of vices (pride, greed, wrath, envy, lust, gluttony and sloth) within Christian teachings. These can be overcome with the seven corresponding virtues of humility, charity, patience, kindness, chastity, temperance and diligence.

Are there seven deadly sins that kill engagement? Perhaps similar to the seven deadly sins on which this metaphor is based, they are difficult to pinpoint. They may seem small, insignificant even: more sins of omission than of commission. Accepted as "the way we do things around here", having seeped into the culture, making it difficult to even identify them as "sins".

They may not be deliberate, but that doesn't mean that cumulatively they are not deadly – because the end result is that they kill engagement. By not seeing them clearly, leaders risk missing their greatest opportunity: to transform their five, fifty or fifty thousand reluctant employees into five, fifty, fifty thousand fans!

Let's switch to a more positive note: while many of us may have heard of the seven deadly sins, I would hazard a guess that their seven corresponding virtues are less well known. And yet, while it's important to see and clearly identify what is wrong (the sin) – what then? Identifying what's right, what to focus on, what to build, where to develop, is a far more useful activity.

That is the spirit and intent of this book: to shine a light on the seven sins that kill engagement, but more importantly to identify seven secrets, seven guideposts that leaders can focus on to foster engagement. What's more, each of these seven secrets is backed by solid multi-disciplinary scientific evidence (from the fields of neuroscience, psychology, behavioural economics) which prove their efficacy in terms of enhancing levels of motivation and productivity.

While the next section will make the case for each sin and its corresponding secret, part two and part three of this book focus on how leaders can put the seven secrets into practice as they lead themselves and others.

The Seven Sins and Seven Secrets

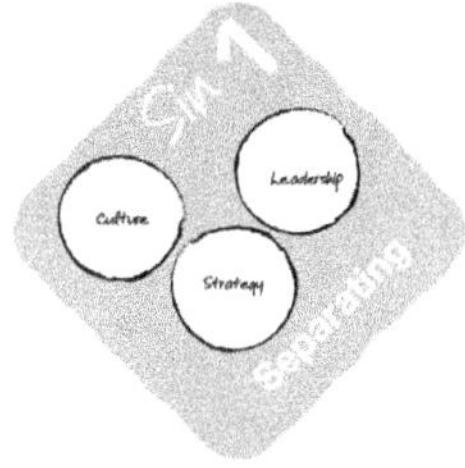

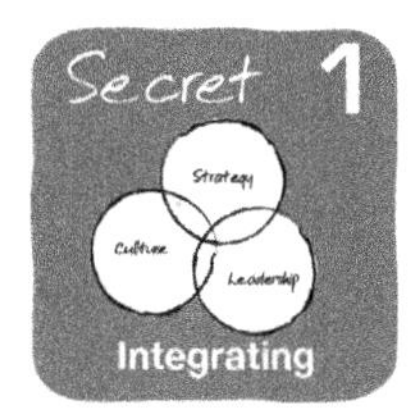

Separating strategy, culture and leadership | rather than | Integrating strategy, culture and leadership

Overwhelming employees with detail and complexity | rather than | Simplifying and making meaning in the context of the big picture

Sending Out Stuff (SOS-ing) | rather than | Encouraging dialogue and discussion, which are the oxygen of change

Secret 4
Pursuing Alignment

Pursuing agreement and consensus

rather than

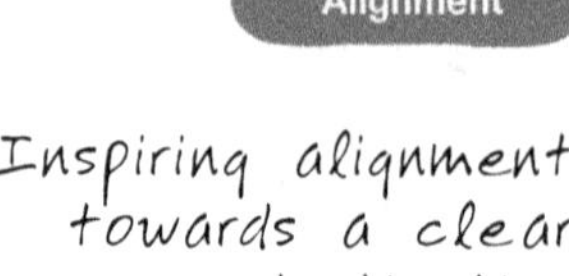

Inspiring alignment towards a clear destination

Jargonising (letting buzzwords run riot)

rather than

Using business stories that are concrete, impactful, memorable and sticky

Secret 6
Authenticity

Hero-worshipping role models

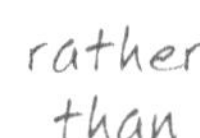

rather than

Being authentic

Speaking

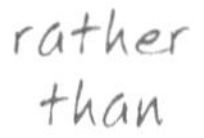

rather than

Listening

Treating strategy, culture and leadership as ***separate disciplines*** *rather than* ***integrating*** *them in a practical way that empowers employees at all levels.*

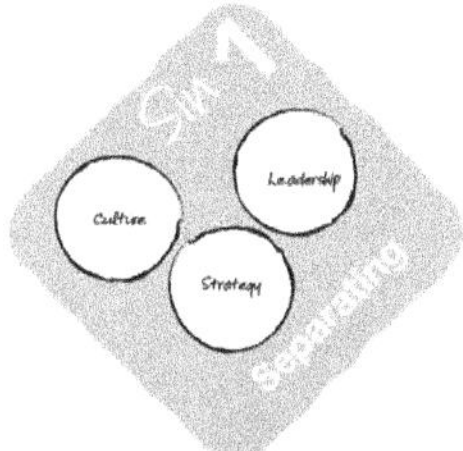

rather than

Strategy, culture and leadership are the three significant levers that leaders have at their disposal to positively influence engagement. Faced with growing uncertainty about the world we operate in, having a strategic plan makes leaders and consequently their followers, feel a little more in control.

Likewise embarking on a culture transformation initiative reassures employees that it's possible to create a great culture that will drive business performance. And as far as leadership development is concerned, it's universally acknowledged as an essential lever – and often even outsourced to an external, academically revered institution.

Let's take a closer look at each of these three areas.

Figure 1: Model showing integration of strategy, culture and leadership. Source: THINKspiration

Strategy

There are dozens of definitions of strategy. At THINKspiration (our consultancy business) we define strategy as "the set of decisions we make regarding how to allocate scarce resources (time, people, money) to achieve our desired future, given our unique (i.e., differentiating) strengths". Purpose, the question around why companies exist and the difference that they aspire to make to our world, is an integral part of the strategy conversation.

Most companies, convinced that they need a strategy (and they certainly do), plan an annual strategic planning session, which often takes place off-site. They pin their hopes on these two or three days, predicated on the idea that they will emerge with powerful ideas about how to be better, how to entrench competitive advantage, and how to oust the competition.

How's that working out?

However, despite periodically nodding to colleagues, crunching on peppermints and agreeing that the off-site has been a "good session", when the thick dossier arrives a few weeks later, things have moved on.

Later, feedback from the CEO roadshow is disappointing, indicating that most employees can't recall major aspects of the strategy and don't seem to perceive its relevance in terms of what's in it for them. Senior management, believing that action rather than talk will do the trick, put their faith in a plan to cascade goals department by department, hoping that this will result in an aligned organisation.

But it doesn't. Despite an elaborate and time-consuming process of goal alignment, not much changes in terms of engagement, discretionary effort and, subsequently, performance. It's business as usual – and as far as addressing short-term performance expectations, no doubt the bonus scheme will need to kick in! The sad reality of the situation is that the real potential of the strategy to directly affect performance, to turbocharge engagement by connecting with employees' "what's in it for me"(WIIFM) remains dormant.

> The real potential of the strategy to directly affect performance, to turbocharge engagement remains dormant

Culture

"Culture eats strategy for breakfast" is one of the business sayings of our time. The implication that a strong culture trumps a mediocre strategy has pushed culture into the limelight. Suddenly values and culture statements pop up everywhere, adorning boardroom walls, reception areas, even email signatures. Key rings, access cards and tattoos carry their message. I've even seen them displayed behind toilet doors!

There's little doubt as to the significance and impact of culture. Companies with strong cultures are associated with strong financial results: the average increase for firms with strong culture show 756% increase in net income growth over an eleven-year period.[9] But what's the secret to making a company's desired culture a reality?

Culture is found in what leaders do, not what brochures say

While strategy helps us make meaning of the work we do, culture is about how it feels to do it. Culture is "the way we do things around here". It's every employee's daily experience of life lived in the organisation. At THINKspiration we call these the "unwritten rules". These cut to the reality of the culture which is so often in stark contrast to the pretty words on glossy posters.

Unfortunately it's often a case of "never the twain shall meet"! During the late 1990s, my second year of work as a strategic planner at a leading South African advertising agency, I had an exciting offer: a promotional move to South Africa's number one agency, complete with my own portfolio of blue-chip brands.

I remember my interview clearly, beautiful Cape Dutch style premises… the gorgeous colour-coded corporate identity, complete with a cute, exquisitely written booklet called *What we do and how we do it*. This agency was all about "the brand" and it was clear that they lived by this credo (or so I thought at the time). So, despite having been part of a great team that had really fostered my growth during the previous year, I decided to take the plunge and move on.

As expected, the first few weeks felt odd. Mostly because having been used to working in a close-knit team, now I was a lone ranger. There were other planners, but all of us functioned independently. That close sense of belonging that, in hindsight, had nurtured me and brought out the best in me, didn't exist.

The offices were great though, and the clients, the best of breed. I suppressed my niggly sense of uncertainty and soldiered on.

My first big assignment was to lead the brand strategy review for one of the agency's oldest clients, an independent radio station that had been a client since its inception. My immediate boss, Steve, suggested that I have an informal chat with the agency CEO to get his thoughts. After all, he was the creator of this very successful brand.

I was nervous but excited as I entered his gorgeous corner office, complete with views of the Magaliesberg – I was about to meet one of the legends of the industry in person. Nothing could have prepared me for what happened next.

Brusquely demanding to know, "Why are you here and what do you want?" he didn't even give me a chance to speak before launching into a tirade accusing me of not following process and of wasting his time in writing "this little book" (the one that had so impressed me at the interview), which he proceeded to throw at me as he chased me out of his office.

I learnt the hard way, as most of us have, that no matter how glossy the brochures or how pithy the sayings, culture – "what it feels like to work here" – is determined by leaders' actions. My reaction to that incident was visceral – if I could have walked out there and then I would have. I couldn't and didn't, but every single day I remained after that was an epic struggle.

no matter how glossy the brochures or how pithy the sayings, culture – "what it feels like to work here" – is determined by leaders' actions.

I didn't yet know about the concept of engagement, but looking back, I went from passionate and all-in for the company to completely disengaged. I got through it by focusing on my work and my clients, and as often happens, staying while gritting my teeth was the right decision for me. I learned a lot, not least that culture is real and alive and to be found in what leaders do, not in what brochures say.

Marcus Buckingham and Ashley Goodall refer to the bright, shiny, dazzling stuff I experienced during my interview as "cultural plumage" – just like birds, it's what we notice and are attracted to.[10] But that CEO's behaviour, and my experience of it at that company and within that (non) team – that is culture. That is what influenced my performance, my behaviour and ultimately my decision to leave.

It's clear that my experience at the Big Fancy advertising agency came about because of the unwritten rules that drove the culture. In fact, when I 'fessed up to my boss, Steve, he said, "Oh, don't worry about it. The CEO does that to all the newbies, so they'll know their place. It's a rite of passage!" Indeed, but it was one that wasn't adequately captured in the repository of glossy little documents I received as part of my induction.

And that's the chasm organisations languish in: defined on one side by lots of inspirational words, and on the other by leaders at all levels going about their business, in exactly the way they always have.

To be clear, I have nothing against the inspirational and aspirational words that delineate "the company we want to become". I believe that formulating a "culture blueprint" is a key facet of a company's imagined future. Writing it up is the easy part – it's getting leaders to make it come alive that is the real challenge.

Then there's the darker side of culture, which is often easier to identify. As Sasol executives got to grips with their disastrous Lake Charles debacle in 2020, which nearly sank the entire company, it was widely reported in the press that a culture of fear had silenced those who had identified issues and flaws. They were apparently too afraid of the repercussions to speak up.

Often a change in culture becomes a strategic imperative. What to change may be glaringly obvious. How to change it? Not so much.

Leadership

Whenever I ask an audience, "Who are the leaders here?" whether it's in a church, community or business context, less than 5% usually raise their hands. We are brainwashed into believing that leadership is defined by a job title, a position on the organogram or maybe even a reserved parking spot!

This is sheer and utter nonsense! Being a leader is about two things: influence and followers. If you have the will and ability to influence one other human – you are a leader! If people consult you for advice, input, guidance – you have followers! We all lead ourselves, our families, and even our friends.

Being a leader is about two things: influence and followers.

How many times during a social coffee with a friend do we have an opportunity to influence – sometimes simply by listening, sometimes by asking an appropriate question, sometimes by sharing a story? You could replace "social coffee with a friend" with business meeting, family dinner conversation, or chat during the school lift.

From a corporate perspective, if global spend is anything to go by, companies have pinned their hopes on leadership, or more specifically leadership training – which commands a spend of approximately $14 billion globally.[11]

Companies are intoxicated with leadership as a "thing" – a big academic, theoretical thing. They fixate on the set of perfect leadership traits (and which leaders exhibit them), and on the different models of leadership (situational, collaborative, etc.). This is not wrong, but it's not very helpful either. It just doesn't seem to be taking us forward. Because leaders drive engagement. And so, having spent so much, and trained so many leaders globally, why do the engagement numbers look as dismal as they do?

Leaders drive engagement.

Where is your leading leading to?

Leading is action-oriented, not theoretical. It happens in every moment, in every meeting, in every conversation – especially those informal ones at the coffee station, the water cooler, or heaven forbid, the restroom. It happens at every level of every company.

The question for companies is not about how much they spend on leadership development, but rather: "Where is your leading leading to?" In other words, how are leaders at all levels equipped to lead towards the corporate strategy and the aspirational culture on a daily basis?

What tools do they have that are specific to the organisation's strategy and culture? How equipped are they to hold conversations with their team members - discussing and debating the subtleties, the paradoxes, the decisions about where the organisation is going, its choices en route, what the journey will feel like?

So, where does treating strategy, culture and leadership as three separate disciplines really get us?

So, where does treating strategy, culture and leadership as three separate disciplines really get us?

In terms of strategy? A comprehensive, complex PowerPoint slide deck and/or strategy document; perhaps some alignment of goals and measurements (on paper).

In terms of culture? Words on walls, words in glossy brochures – words, words and more words!

In terms of leadership? A level of theoretical knowledge, perhaps some personal development, a certificate.

It's precisely this approach of treating strategy, culture and leadership as separate disciplines that makes it impossible for leaders to put them into practice – and make them come to life.

The reality is that every day, thousands of leaders like Lorna, Sibongile and Willem wake up with the best intention of creating an environment that brings out the best in their people and which positively impacts on performance. Then life happens: a safety crisis, a request from Head Office for an additional urgent report, a crusher that has broken down, a client that is about to pull their business. Nothing could be further from their minds than leading towards strategy and culture. They probably are not even consciously aware of their leading.

They go through their day giving off a slew of culture messages through their micro-behaviours. These tiny signals have disproportionate impact on their teams, because the power of role modelling means that the teams closely observe and frequently emulate what their superiors/role models do and say.

The "rubber hits the road" opportunities to reinforce, or even re-interpret strategy or culture messages simply don't occur to them. Why would they? Because for leaders like Lorna, Sibongile and Willem, strategy and culture are abstract concepts, free-floating somewhere in the vicinity of head office. They do not have the tools or the skills required to make them relevant to daily operational matters – or to discuss them with their team.

Integrating strategy, culture and leadership – the leader's SIM card

Leaders need tools that help them to integrate strategy and culture into their daily operational decisions and activities. They need skills that help them to lead authentically, build relationships, connect, convince and persuade. They need to develop their ability to distil what is relevant to their teams (simplify), to listen and to make their messages stick.

But most of all, leaders need to flip their thinking: instead of thinking about strategy and culture as concepts they need to "sell", they need to start by understanding where their people are, and connect the key elements of the exciting story of the company's future (purpose, strategic outcomes, culture) to employees' WIIFM in a relevant and meaningful way.

Starting with the user experience has transformed the technology industry. Leaders can no longer continue leading without a SIM card – in this case the Simplifying, Integrating and Making sense "software" that would equip them to interact with their team about strategy and culture in a meaningful way. The dismal engagement data tells us so!

Leaders can no longer continue leading without a SIM card

I can't lead for engagement if I don't know where I am "leading to" in terms of strategy and culture.

#2

Overwhelming *employees with* ***complexity*** *and detail* ***(the what)*** *and* ***omitting*** *the big picture, purpose and meaning* ***(the why)****.*

rather than

Another day… (Yet) another initiative!

Most organisations, despite their best intentions to positively affect and influence employee performance, suffer from initiative overload. There's a scene in Monty Python's classic movie, *In Search of the Holy Grail*, that makes me think of life in many corporates: in a fairly middle-class Irish household we see the very pregnant lady of the house ironing away, seemingly unperturbed by the literally hundreds of children that are crawling out from every nook and cranny, perched upon the bookcases and hanging from the lampshades. The soundtrack leaves one in no doubt that "every sperm is sacred", as she later sings, much like every initiative from head office!

And there's no shortage of initiatives out there. Indeed, one of the unspoken truths of corporate life is how disorienting – if not outright bewildering – it often is. One minute you are in a meeting about the new operating model. Then it's annual strategic planning time again. What about the revised incentive scheme? And then there's the culture transformation initiative that needs your input. In the meantime, the planning for the annual exco roadshow has become urgent. What about the team-building session to address team dysfunctionality?

Seeing the big picture

Humans are meaning-making machines. We want to understand, to join the dots, to see the big picture and know how we fit into it. But in most companies, employees only see a few pieces of the puzzle. One piece says "innovate", another says "cut costs", another says "go fast", another says "go slow".

None of these pieces make sense, because what's missing is the picture on the lid of the puzzle box

None of these pieces make sense, because what's missing is the picture on the lid of the puzzle box – the big picture that shows how the puzzle pieces fit together. Leaders forget that the closer they are to the top of the structure, the more likely they are to have a puzzle box/big picture view – but lower down the structure, employees only have the individual pieces. And while these puzzle piece initiatives may be well intentioned, and may even be well implemented, in the absence of a big picture, they most likely result in confusion and frustration.

We have lost the plot

And this is where our obsession with using a PowerPoint slide deck and its commensurate list of bullet points substantially exacerbates the problem. If we think of corporate strategy as a story of the future we want to create, it would be safe to say that it's a story in which we really and truly have lost the plot.

As Jeff Bezos has commented regarding his decision to outlaw PowerPoint presentations in 2004: "PowerPoint is far too easy a medium in which to deposit a set of unrelated and incoherent bullet points... whereas a narrative structure demands coherence and logic." Instead, he requires everyone at Amazon to write a one-page narrative to make their point. To do this, the writer has to coherently formulate his/her "plot", i.e., how one point is related to another. It's these vital "join the dots" links that are the sense makers and which fire up the audience's brain.[12]

It's a leader's job to join the dots, to translate, to distil the company's strategic choices into a compelling story. Against this backdrop, leaders should discuss with employees the inevitable complex web of initiatives required to take the company towards who and what it wants to become.

You can't open an annual report or visit a corporate website without tripping over the concept of purpose. And as much as I dislike buzzwords, I think that purpose has a significant role to play in fixing the world of work, and changing it for the better.

Because purpose is big picture, it helps us to focus on the whole. Purpose is about meaning. It provides the "why", and makes the detail, the myriad of initiatives, make sense.

The idea of purpose is not new. Before the Industrial Revolution (circa 1850), a farmer would work the land to feed his family. He would literally see (and eat) the results of his labour. A cobbler would personally interact with his customer, touch and measure his foot, understand his need and make something to satisfy the customer's specific requirements. Purpose was inextricably linked to the work process.

Enter the Industrial Revolution, which focused on scale, repetition, and efficiency, its objective being to systematically break work down into its smallest viable components. The result? Repetitive tasks performed with efficiency. Except that by breaking work down into a series of repetitive and compartmentalised tasks, the connection to the end product was severed. The purpose and meaning of it all, i.e., the food on the table or the shoe on the customer's foot, was lost.

So now, big corporates like Nike and Tiger Brands have replaced the cobbler and farmer. These big corporations consist of thousands of people whose work is broken down into minuscule sets of scripted and repetitive tasks.

There are jobs that consist purely of the negotiation of the price of shoelaces. These employees never see the shoe – they don't even run. There are call centre operators making call after call (fifty to sixty times a day) according to the same script; miners drilling hole after hole underground. Almost every job in the world has been broken down into tiny, little, repeatable activities, activities that are in and of themselves devoid of meaning and purpose – the very things that make life worth living and work worth doing!

Even if the design and structure of work itself falls beyond their sphere of influence, leaders can improve employee engagement by connecting the dots between detailed operational activities and the organisation's overarching purpose.

I can't lead for engagement if I overwhelm employees with complexity rather than simplifying and making meaning for them.

***Sending out stuff (S.O.S)** rather than encouraging **dialogue** and **discussion,** which are the oxygen of change.*

rather than

Over the past 20 years, organisational communication has not only failed to improve, it is actually getting worse. Kaplan and Norton's notorious finding that 95% of employees have no idea of their company's strategy is much cited and sadly corroborated: according to Watson Wyatt Worldwide only 40% of managers have a clear understanding of their company's strategy.[13 14]

This problem affects organisations, even at the highest levels – research at MIT showed that only 28% of executives in executive teams could correctly identify the strategic priorities of their organisations.[15]

These statistics are baffling when we consider the time, resources and money thrown around in the name of communication. Companies will proudly tell you about the 600-word e-mail that gets sent out weekly, the executive road show, the one hundred-slide PowerPoint strategy presentation, and the WhatsApp clip from the CEO - all available on the company intranet. This is the stuff we send out that assuages our consciences, but seemingly accomplishes little else!

I remember chatting to Gill*, the then head of strategy and corporate communication at one of our large ICT companies, some years ago. This was a maverick brand, which had just appointed a pioneering new CEO. After many weeks of PowerPoint road shows (complete with glossy leave-behind) to the deepest, darkest corners of the country, Gill had, a few weeks later, called in some of her senior regional managers to get some feedback.

These statistics are baffling when we consider the time, resources and money thrown around in the name of communication.

According to Gill, "There was a deathly silence, followed by some sheepish flipping through said brochures." The bottom line, after all that time, money, energy and effort was that, even among senior managers, no one remembered a thing. "I'm at my wits end," Gill lamented. "What on earth do we have to do to get employees to get the message?"

To answer Gill, companies need to do two things that may sound simple, but in reality are far from easy. The first one requires a mindset shift, an acknowledgement that companies do not "own" their employees.

They cannot tell them how things are going to be via lists and lists of bullet points. (Well, they can, but refer to the above paragraphs to see how that's working out!) Employees have a choice: to listen, to understand and to act.

So, much like external marketers do, companies need to think of their employees as internal target audiences. They need to understand employees' needs, their triggers, their WIIFMs – and shape and design their messages and conversations accordingly.

The second thing requires businesses to heed how we as human beings process and internalise information: we talk about it.

Dialogue is the oxygen of change

Research shows repeatedly that dialogue is the oxygen of change and that it is only once we have talked about a concept or idea, turned it over in our minds, discussed it – and come to our own conclusions – that we start to own and internalise it.[16]

What this means is that the everyday water cooler, coffee station, and changing room conversations are far more impactful than the dazzling PowerPoint roadshows that drain both time and money. Leaders should be asking how they can influence changing room, corridor, water cooler conversations; how they can shift from presentations to conversations? How can they speak less and get employees to talk more, or ask questions that orchestrate a series of a-ha moments?

Unless leaders are deliberate about changing this, the S.O.S deluge will continue. And the vital ideas of purpose, strategy, culture, values (albeit painstakingly word-smithed at an exotic off-site location) will continue to languish somewhere in a corner office, while employees – unaware of any connection between what they do and the company's direction – grow increasingly disengaged and demoralised.

I can't lead for engagement if I have merely sent out stuff rather than creating the opportunity for employees to discuss and internalise the message.

Pursuing ***agreement*** *and* ***consensus*** *regarding strategic choices rather than* ***inspiring alignment*** *towards a clear destination.*

rather than

"If you want everyone to like you, sell ice cream: don't try and be a leader." So says a wise friend and client who is leading a mining business through radical changes. Another oft quoted truism is: "Leadership is not a popularity contest."

Leadership is about picking a direction, and often making some tough (and unpopular) decisions about how to reach that true north. While agreement speaks to consensus, alignment speaks to direction. Like a magnet, alignment towards something attracts. It's up to the leader to clarify the ultimate destination, the purpose of the trip (the why) and the route that has been decided upon (the strategy).

Leadership is about picking a direction, and often making some tough decisions about how to reach that true north.

Waze or Google Maps are good metaphors for corporate strategy: there's a group of people/employees who want to go somewhere. There's a purpose to their trip, but until their destination, their true north, has been decided, there are no options in terms of route or resources. Once that destination is captured, however, the algorithm will offer several options depending on conditions along the way.

Once all travellers are on board, there may be disagreements – about how many stops, what music to listen to etc. There may even be disagreements about the route (I mean who of us haven't at some point overruled the Waze algorithm – and lived to regret it!). But ultimately, it's the driver's call.

It's their decision, but that doesn't mean that they don't entertain discussion, conversation, or offer some explanations for the decision. It also doesn't mean that everything they do is clear cut.

The driver may make trade-offs when it comes to time and preferred route. They may want to avoid dodgy or dangerous environments. Some of these trade-offs or paradoxes may mystify the passengers, but the driver doesn't remain silent. They talk about these decisions. Similarly, in companies, there may be trade-offs and decisions that seem at odds with each other.

How to explain capital expenditure and cost cutting happening simultaneously? Recruiting new employees for certain functions and retrenching others? What about the age-old safety vs. production paradox endemic to the resources industry?

Leaders that seek agreement would rather not discuss these paradoxes. They feel stymied because they don't have all the "right" answers. However these paradoxes are real, and by not talking about them (in pursuit of agreement) leaders harm their own credibility, foster mistrust and miss a golden opportunity for alignment. Most importantly, leaders miss the chance to expand their employees' thinking from "either/or" to understanding and accepting the need for "both/and".

Leaders need to get comfortable with not having all the answers.

Leaders need to get comfortable with not having all the answers

Trade-offs or paradoxes are the lifeblood of every business. Ignoring them doesn't make them go away, it just creates more confusion.

I have often reflected on the deathly silence that leaders frequently face after presentations. "No questions? Good!" Here's the thing: "No questions" is no good! No questions doesn't mean that everyone agrees. It means that people are afraid to voice their opinions, or satisfy their curiosity, or speak up.

Leaders are comfortable with "no questions" because it feels like agreement. It feels like "job done, tick the box". And so they stop short of aligning a disparate group of employees towards the picture of an exciting future, for the business and for them as individuals.

Leaders need to welcome diversity, and simultaneously be crystal clear on alignment. Aligning a diverse employee contingent towards the company's true north enables all employees to see and own the whole. How does this work? Well, think for a moment about the HR executive who is championing culture, the IT executive pushing digitisation, the operations executive who never stops talking about production, the safety executive who's focused on improving safety stats.

Each of these initiatives is vitally important to the business – however, if not clarified in the context of the whole, the direction, they result in confusion. Alignment means that all leaders bear responsibility for owning the whole picture on the puzzle box lid rather than just their own part of the puzzle.

I can't lead for engagement and inspire employees towards an exciting future if I am not clear about our destination.

Allowing ***buzzwords*** *to* ***run riot****, rather than using* ***business stories*** *that are* ***concrete****, impactful, and memorable.*

rather than

Words create worlds. They are powerful tools that should help us to clarify and inspire: to describe a compelling future of the business we dream of creating and of the difference we feel called to make. Unfortunately, the language predominating in the business world does anything but that.

Not only do abstract terms like "operational efficiency", "competitive advantage", "leveraging downstream operations", "economies of scale", and "synergies" trigger a yawn fest – they add to the confusion rather than clarify it. And yet we revere this professional business language, believing that these big words, this business school jargon, makes us sound smart and rational. Many blue-chip outfits' glossary of terms and acronyms extend well beyond fifty pages!

As well as exacerbating confusion, business jargon also wastes precious time: I recall sitting through many endless meetings with well-meaning colleagues where we tried to pin down terms like vision, mission, values – to bring them to heel once and for all – and leaving exhausted, confused and feeling more hogtied than ever.

According to George Bernard Shaw, "the biggest problem with communication is the illusion that it has taken place". When communication has indeed taken place successfully the result is shared meaning between sender and receiver. And yet, there's nothing shared and little meaning in the abstract "language of business" that we speak.

Buzzwords and jargon grease the wheels of confusion! These overused, meaningless phrases anaesthetise us into not even bothering to ask for clarification. If only we were able to tally up the costs involved in "unshared" meaning: the lack of alignment to the strategy, the misdirected initiatives, the general chaos and confusion. If you think you have created shared meaning and understanding around your strategy you would be among a tiny minority (according to Harvard Business School Professors Collis and Ruckstad.)[17] Could you summarise your company's strategy in two or three sentences? If so, would your colleagues put it the same way?

Buzzwords and jargon grease the wheels of confusion!

Business language/jargon may be uninspiring, and may cause confusion, but its fundamental problem is that because it's abstract and non-specific, it's difficult to remember. What mental picture does "operational efficiency" trigger? Or how about this statement: "Our product integrates digital systems and orientates you towards re-imagination so that innovation is not restricted"? A big fat blank space is the only picture I'm getting.

It doesn't have to be this way! Imagine if leaders replaced hackneyed, overused business jargon with words – imaginative, creative and brave words about the company's future that could mobilise minds, inspire souls and touch hearts. Martin Luther

King did it when he talked about having a dream (please note he didn't have a KPI or even a plan!). Apple did it with their 1997 advertisement, "Here's to the crazy ones". It was an ode not to computers or technology but to a mindset, an attitude, a tribute to those square pegs in round holes – the "crazy ones" – who push the human race forward, who believe they can change the world, and who are the ones that do.[18]

Imagine if JFK had said: "By collaborating we will leverage our competitive advantage and endeavour to succeed by creating an opportunity, potentially for homo sapiens to traverse soil somewhere in our vast galaxy, in the foreseeable future." Thankfully, his words were far more pithy and concrete: "We will put a man on the moon before the end of the decade."[19]

That statement is memorable, not least of all because we can visualise it happening. It presents a "mini Netflix" moment. It's a micro-story. And it's stories that make the abstract concrete, and messages memorable, impactful and sticky. How? Because when we hear a business story we can visualise it happening.

This example makes the point: most companies have "integrity" as one of their values, along with an equally abstract and unmemorable (but impressive) list of bullet points. In contrast, allow me to tell you about a time, a couple of years ago when I visited a mining client at their offices in Carletonville. As I signed in, I was struck by the friendly security guard Jabulani (which means happiness) who helped me as I struggled through the turnstile with my multitudes of bags and posters. Little did I realise that during this process my wallet fell out of my open handbag. None the wiser, I completed my presentation and was greeted on my way out by a beaming Jabulani, delighted to be able to hand me back my wallet (with every note and credit card intact), before I had even missed it. Now that's integrity!

Could you picture Lorna, the emancipated banker who no longer has to worry about "who is going to destroy me today?" Or Gill, my frustrated corporate communication client who I mentioned a few pages ago? No doubt you could. Business stories take us to events that we can see happening in our mind's eye, trigger an emotional response and book a spot in our memory banks. They are powerful weapons of persuasion and trump fancy jargon every time!

I can't lead for engagement if my message doesn't stick.

Aspiring** to be the "next... (Steve Jobs/Elon Musk/ Jeff Bezos)..." rather than being brave enough to **be ourselves.

rather than

Holding out for a hero

Many South Africans have a "Madiba (Nelson Mandela) moment" – when we met him, were close to him or felt his life-changing presence, even if from afar. Mine was at the Cape Town Stadium at the inaugural 46664 concert. My husband, Bernard, and I were sitting a few rows behind him in the VIP box. Bernard had met Madiba on a few occasions – for me, no such luck!

As the proceedings were about to begin, Madiba turned around, caught Bernard's eye, acknowledged him with a nod and raised his water bottle in greeting to me. Such a small gesture, but immediately I felt a connection. In a way it was a perfect moment – I was close enough to bask in the Madiba magic, without reality threatening to intrude and destroy my illusion.

Madiba, Barack Obama, Warren Buffett, Bill Gates, Steve Jobs, Richard Branson, Elon Musk. When we think "leadership" these are the names that come to mind. We deify their words, actions and ideas. We build them up into superhuman versions of themselves – study their backgrounds, educations, reading lists, even Spotify playlists.

For the most part, they are the first to admit that they are just as human as we are. But we don't like to hear that. We want them to be more. We need them to be more. Why? Perhaps because they are a beautiful distraction: if we keep focusing on reading what Bill reads, listening to what Barack listens to (smoking what Elon smokes?!), we keep the focus on what's "out there", rather than – heaven forbid – what's going on "in here". It also happens to be the perfect excuse, maybe even cop-out, for not leading… after all, "I am not Madiba," we tell ourselves!

Over the years, I've been privileged to work closely with business leaders, many of whom occupy the top job. The title, corner office and hefty remuneration often obscure the realities that come as part of the package.

Unending pressure to perform and drive other people's performance. Stress. Fear of failure. Negotiating politics, complexities, and ambiguities… all of which must be fearlessly faced down. It's not quite an environment conducive to the boss being vulnerable and authentic. It's far safer to practice tried and trusted rule-by-fear, blame and shame-style leadership. To do it ourselves rather than risk anyone else doing it imperfectly. To seek refuge in cynicism, sarcasm or emotional stoicism.

Some of these tactics may even work over the short term. They may deliver "results", but they don't create followers, or engaged fans. They don't inspire people to grow into the best versions of themselves. And yet even though we know its shortcomings,

> We cling to the ideal of the strong, fearless leader – because we battle to get our heads around the alternative. Being authentic, being vulnerable, being me!

we cling to the ideal of the strong, fearless leader – perhaps because we battle to get our heads around the alternative. Being authentic, being vulnerable, being me!

Fear: our Operating System (OS)

It's easier to hide behind a title, a job description, a persona. Being me is scary. There's no template, no outfit, car, or neighbourhood I can live in. There's no authenticity playbook.

Why is being authentic especially at work so challenging? Because we literally live and work in fear. Fear of not delivering. Fear of making a mistake. Fear of being discovered as the imposters we suspect ourselves to be.

How do we deal with all this fear? We take control. We armour up. We make sure that we put on our take-no-prisoners attitude, our sarcasm or our perfectionism first thing every morning. We work hard, and sometimes wheel, deal, and politick with the best of them all in the name of getting ahead. We never let the real us – the mother, father, sister, daughter that our friends and family love and admire – be seen behind our mask.

The more we can control the less we have to fear. Right? It's no wonder that command and control style leadership with POLC (plan, organise, lead, control) as its wingman have become the way we do things. Required by the environment to be tough, Kevlar-plated stormtroopers, we check in our humanity every time we clock-in. Removing the "human" from humanity leaves us as "ity" bitty versions of who we are really meant to be.

We truly believe that when we get to the top, when we have the power, that somehow this will get easier, will feel better. It doesn't. We don't realise that more power just feeds its own insatiability and makes us so fearful of losing it, that we will do anything to keep it. Turbocharged by fear, and already accustomed to suppressing our humanity, we start to see and treat employees as a means to our end, as pawns in our game of winning at all costs, so that we can deliver to shareholders, rack up record profits and somehow hold on.

The power disease

Keltner talks about the "power disease" that affects each and every one of us. This is how it works: once we get into a position of power (often driven by fear) we become laser-focused on doing everything possible to keep that power. So, a lot of things that we do when we are at home with friends and family (like listening, appreciation, trust, respect, recognition, gratitude) fly out of the window.[20]

This power disease means that we start to see others as means to accomplish our end. We dehumanise them and see the worst in them. "They" are lazy, greedy, incompetent, uneducated… Whatever! Of course, what you look for you find, and so the cycle perpetuates: we find ourselves wondering what to do to get these lazy, greedy, incompetent "workers" to be productive? To work safely? To be engaged?

Who we are is how we lead: Authenticity and connection

Power moves leaders further away from those they lead. It estranges them from employees. It hinders engagement. It distorts connection. What's the vaccine for the power disease? Authenticity!

What's the vaccine for the power disease? Authenticity!

The great news for leaders is that they don't have to be perfect. But they do have to be authentic. Be themselves. Be brave enough to be vulnerable. Be okay with letting themselves be seen in all their imperfect glory. Regularly and deliberately demonstrate what they don't know, what they are scared of, what disappoints them.

Maybe this makes you cringe (let's face it – it makes most of us cringe). But if leaders want to connect with their followers, authenticity and vulnerability are non-negotiable. Brené Brown talks about authenticity and vulnerability as the birthplace of connection.[21] Connection, the essence of the relationship between a leader and his/her followers, is the holy grail of leadership.

I can't lead for engagement if I can't connect authentically with my employees.

Speaking *most of the time rather than* **listening.**

rather than

As a society we know how to talk. TED talks, Twitter, Toastmasters, Professional Speaking Associations all indicate that as a society we value talking. Schools train and encourage pupils to hone their skills in public speaking. Public (or even private!) listening? Not so much!

The workplace entrenches this disparity. One CEO I know, when espousing the value of listening, a skill he says he regrettably only learned later in his leadership journey, says: "I was promoted because I knew how to talk, not because I knew how to listen."

Leaders in the workplace are groomed to lead the conversation, to present, to chair meetings. When it comes to leadership, our "speak first" paradigm means that we mistakenly evaluate leaders on what comes out of their mouths, rather than how they use their ears, (eyes and hearts) to listen for feelings and sense what underlies behaviour.

Perhaps leaders fear that if they shut up and listen, others might think they don't know what to say or do. Or, that they may lose an opportunity to stamp their authority or make their mark?

I've had many conversations about listening with leaders. (The irony is not lost on me!). Those less predisposed to "listen first" seem to be of the opinion that that although there's nothing wrong with listening, it's merely a nice-to-have (if you have the time) for leaders. Surely as a leader, having scaled the corporate hierarchy you are liberated from hearing about other people's opinions? Especially those who don't really have a say? (Sarcasm alert here!)

Don't be a know-it-all

Leaders need to shrug off the know-it-all mantle and become a lot more obsessed with asking the right questions rather than having the right answers.

In 2011, we made the pilgrimage to the legendary Berkshire Hathaway AGM in Omaha. Known as the "Woodstock of capitalism", it's a 40 000 people event, held in a basketball stadium, where Berkshire Hathaway's two "rock stars" (major shareholders) Warren Buffett and Charlie Munger hold court by answering questions for upwards of five hours. Despite Omaha being a bit of a dump, the five-hour AGM had its memorable moments. My highlight was the unforgettable Charlie Munger (then 91), alternately chewing his way through boxes of Sees Candy, sleeping through the more boring parts, and showing off his razor-sharp wit and his absolute inability to suffer fools gladly.

One of the characteristics of the 40 000 strong spectacle is the opportunity for audience members to put questions directly to Warren and Charlie. But you know those questions that are really a CV camouflaged as a question? Well, one young lady from California did not hold back in her supposed question to Charlie Munger, and after what felt like ten minutes listing every accomplishment on her CV, she eventually landed on a form of a question, ending with, "Charlie, what would you do?"

Without skipping a beat, he retorted: "Well my dear, you seem to know it all, I don't know why you are asking me!"

Leaders who seem to know it all or come across as having all the answers immediately shut down engagement. However, I suspect that the paradigm of the all-knowing leader still reigns in some quarters.

Leaders who seem to know it all or come across as having all the answers immediately shut down engagement.

Leaders who are afraid of looking stupid, unqualified, or ignorant have no appetite for messy "I don't know" types of conversations. It's far safer to retreat to their "I speak, you listen" comfort zone.

Great leaders are great listeners

Listening may sound like an optional extra for leaders. It's not. The truth is that leaders who can't listen, can't lead. It's only a leader's ability to listen that can unleash the power of their spoken words. How could a leader reach employees, connect with their issues, appeal to their passions, without knowing anything about them?

Listening may sound like an optional extra for leaders. It's not.

I'll never forget a former client in the mining industry waxing lyrical about the time he spent as a young graduate in the miners' change-house. Miners are traditionally among the lowest levels of the hierarchy and my client (despite the fact that he was on a supersonic trajectory to the top) reckons that this is where he learned the most about the business. "Despite having the most basic of qualifications, these guys knew the business, talked passionately and smartly about its problems and challenges, and what should be done about them," he told me. (Sound like fans to me!) What a pity in that case – and many others – that the soundproofed C-suite remained oblivious!

There's so much to learn, if leaders can replace the need to show how clever they are with genuine curiosity. As well as eliciting incredible insights, listening is without a doubt the first step towards engagement. Finding out what employees are curious about, what confuses them, what they would do if they were in the boss's shoes, kickstarts the engagement process. Leaders, through their questions, encourage employees to think. In fact, the four most empowering words a leader can utter are: "What do you think?"

The four most empowering words a leader can utter are: "What do you think?"

Leaders need to remember that employees are talking about the business all the time: passionately and articulately. Around the watercooler, in the changing room, at the coffee station. It's a leader's job to listen, to tap into these conversations, to understand the issues, and to go to where employees are. Because that is the only way for leaders to take them with to the compelling future of their dreams.

I can't lead for engagement unless I have first listened to my employees.

What now?

The seven Sins

It's clearly evident, both empirically and anecdotally, that the seven sins described above hamper leaders' efforts in connecting with and engaging their employees. To summarise:

Sin 1: Separating

"I can't lead for engagement if I don't know where I am leading to in terms of strategy and culture."

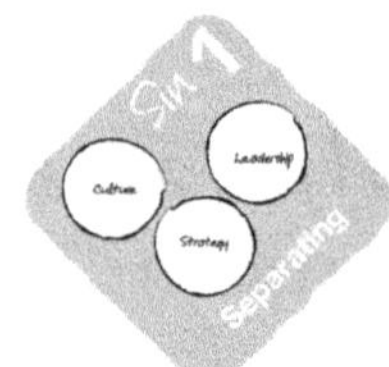

Sin 2: Complicating

"I can't lead for engagement if I overwhelm employees with complexity rather than simplifying and making meaning for them."

Sin 3: Sending Out Stuff

"I can't lead for engagement if I have merely sent out stuff rather than creating the opportunity for employees to discuss and internalise the message."

Sin 4: Pursuing agreement

"I can't lead for engagement and inspire employees towards an exciting future if I am not clear about our destination."

Sin 5: Jargonising

"I can't lead for engagement if my message doesn't stick."

Sin 6: Hero-worshipping

"I can't lead for engagement if I can't connect authentically with my employees."

Sin 7: Speaking

"I can't lead for engagement unless I have first listened to my employees."

The seven Secrets

While the "sins" may be useful in shedding light on the problem – it is the secrets that are far more useful in terms of identifying what works, what to build on, and what skills and tools leaders need to develop. What should leaders address systemically in the companies they steer, and what should they put on their to-do lists each and every day?

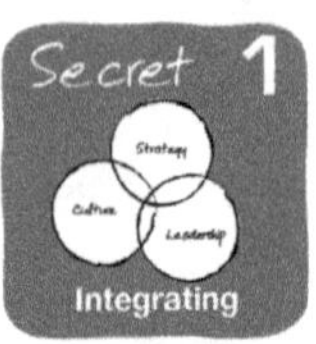

Integrate strategy, culture and leadership and bring these to life on a daily basis.

Simplify and contextualise the detail within the big picture, injecting work with purpose and meaning.

Catalyse interactive discussion, stimulate curiosity and facilitate dialogue.

Align employees towards a chosen direction.

Embrace the power of business stories.

Be authentic.

Listen.

These are the ingredients of successful and effective leadership. By focusing on these principles, every leader (regardless of whether they are leading a team of five or five hundred) can turn employees into fans and leave a leadership legacy to be proud of.

While ingredients are important, a great dish is the result of how one combines them in practice. That is essentially what this book is about. How can leaders effectively lead themselves using these ingredients? And how can they effectively lead others using the same ingredients?

In order to lead THEMSELVES effectively, leaders need to focus on:

- Authenticity (Secret 6) by being brave enough to know themselves, and brave enough to show up as themselves;
- Listening (Secret 7) by learning to shut up and listen first; and
- Storytelling (Secret 5) by using the power of story to connect and influence – ensuring that their messages are memorable, impactful and sticky.

In order to LEAD OTHERS effectively, leaders need to focus on:

- Aligning (Secret 4) by painting an inspiring picture of the future of the business;
- Listening (Secret 7) by finding out where their people are;
- Simplifying (Secret 2) by distilling their strategy (culture and all commensurate initiatives) into a compelling story;
- Integrating (Secret 1) by visualising the story in a way that captures the detail as well as the big picture; and
- Discussion, dialogue (Secret 3) and storytelling (Secret 5) which equip all employees from boardroom to shopfloor with the tools and skills to talk about the exciting story of the future that the company dreams about creating – integrating the company's strategy, culture and leadership initiatives (Secret 1) in a sustainable way.

Leading yourself:

"You can't lead others if you can't lead yourself."

Chapter 1: Be brave enough to know yourself and brave enough to show up as yourself

Looking for leaders in all the wrong places

What does the "perfect" leader look like? Sound like? What defines him/her? It's not as if we don't have lists… and lists… and lists!

As well intentioned as academia is in attempting to enhance our conceptual understanding of leadership, the problem is that our theoretical list of traits exhibited by the perfect leader continues to grow. And as it does, so too does our disillusionment when none of our leaders *du jour* quite measure up. Because the reality is that for every quality on the list, there will always be an iconic leader who lacks it.

Steve Jobs, globally acknowledged as a visionary leader who made more than his dent in the universe was known to buy a new car every six months, avoiding ever registering its licence plates, so that he could never be ticketed for speeding. In that regard, he can hardly be considered a paragon of ethical virtue!

There are stories about Martin Luther King being a notorious womaniser. Madiba himself scorned his deification, calling himself a "sinner trying to do better".

If you are going to be anything, be spiky

Even if we were able to create the ultimate "perfect ten" list for leaders, we would be faced with two problems. First, there's simply no leader that would ever be able to tick all the boxes.

Second, the stark reality is that the most captivating, mesmerising and indeed effective leaders are actually not well-rounded. Quite the contrary, in fact: they are extreme. They are passionate. They use their uniqueness to make their mark on the world. In the words of Buckingham and Goodall, they are spiky.

Spikiness is authenticity made visible

Spikiness is authenticity made visible. And it's to each leader's spikiness that his/her followers attach themselves.[22]

Third, leadership is situational: there are times where a rallying sports captain, turnaround specialist or steadying-the-ship type leadership style may be the most apt and appropriate.

There simply isn't a gold standard, a perfect role model of leadership – there never has been. Rather than role modelling Steve Jobs, Elon Musk, Bill Gates or even Madiba, we need to start the process of becoming the leader WE are really meant to be.

This brings us to the question – what defines a leader? A leader is someone who has followers. Who follow what exactly? Their chosen leader's uniqueness, their specialness, their spikiness. Their passion to make a difference.

So, in the real world, we don't follow a "perfect ten" leader, but we do follow leaders who are the "YOUEST you" (to quote Dr Seuss.)[23]

Why do we follow "spikiness?" Because all of us want to feel part of something bigger than ourselves and because all of us want to feel seen and acknowledged for our individual contribution. This is good sense, and also good science. A leader is defined by what they create in their followers.

Knowing yourself – what are you creating in your followers?

My previous book *The Leadership Riptide and How to Escape* was published in 2016. At its core is my "more/less" model, predicated on the latest research (from multi-disciplinary sources in neuroscience, psychology, behavioural science and economics), that identifies the kind of environments that leaders should create to engage and bring out the best in their followers.[24]

It's clear that engagement is less about the "ideal" leader and more about the environment/s they create. While the science is crystal clear on this, there are noteworthy discrepancies between what science clearly demonstrates and what are still entrenched common practices in business today.

Engagement is less about the "ideal" leader and more about the environment/s they create

This discrepancy forms the basis for my less/more model (diagram below). In it I propose that if we follow the scientific evidence about what motivates and inspires employees, leaders need to focus:

- more on play and less on the drudgery of work;
- more on building trust and less on enforcing compliance;

- more on identifying strengths and less on correcting weaknesses;
- more on love (mastery, autonomy and purpose) and less on incentives to drive behaviour;
- more on the power of progress, and less on the numbers themselves; and
- more on actually putting leading into practice and less on theory of leadership.

Figure 2: The Leadership Riptide more/less model[25]

One of the more frequently asked questions about my book, *The Leadership Riptide and How to Escape* is: "What on earth does leadership have to do with a riptide?" As anyone who has ever had the misfortune to be caught in a riptide will know, you swim frantically, and expend an amazing amount of energy, only to look up and find yourself no closer to the shore. Often, you don't even realise you are actually in a riptide.

As I reflected on the world of work, and the discrepancy between what science knows and what business does, this mental picture of a riptide resonated with me: leaders caught in a riptide, frantically thrashing about, drowning in initiatives and activities, yet no closer to the "shore" of engaged employees.

To escape a riptide, you have to swim differently – and the same holds true here – to escape this "leadership riptide" leaders need to lead differently. Leading differently requires every leader to identify whether he/she is indeed caught in a riptide by asking some tough questions.

As a leader:

- Do you see yourself creating environments of play and experimentation – because they are the catalyst for possibility thinking, problem solving and innovation? Are you able to stimulate curiosity and handle experimentation and its commensurate failures in a psychologically safe way?
- Do you regard trust as the backbone of your business, not just because it increases profitably by a staggering 286%, but because feeling trusted profoundly impacts on employees' sense of autonomy and therefore intrinsic motivation?[26]
- Do you rely on monetary rewards and incentives to motivate employees and influence their behaviour at the expense of creating an environment of mastery, autonomy and purpose (which takes a lot more effort)? Are you deliberate about being a "meaning maker", connecting the drudgery of the daily grind to a higher purpose? Edward Kieswetter (The Commissioner of the South African Revenue Services) talks about how as a young power station manager he realised that his job was to make meaning for his team. He reframed the drudgery of endlessly shovelling coal on a daily basis by helping them to imagine who was on the other end of that shovel of coal: the hospital patient on life support, the township child enabled to finish his homework, the mom able to cook dinner for her family.
- Do you look for the good, recognise your and others' strengths, and focus on what's going right? Are you aware of the merits of a strengths-based culture in terms of profitability, motivation and engagement?[27]

- Do you realise that the power of progress is the most powerful motivator of performance? It's not the goals themselves that pull people, it is the daily small wins and the tiny steps we take towards achieving them that keep people energised and focused. Do you seize every opportunity to focus on the progress your team achieves – infinitesimal as it may seem?
- Finally, have you made the distinction between leadership, a theoretical concept, and leading – a daily practice? My sister Kimmy was a national swimming champion at the age of twelve. As her little sister, having spent many, many hours alongside the swimming pool, I was as well versed as a six-year-old could be in the theory of swimming. So well versed, in fact, that Kimmy's provincial team adopted me as their team mascot, complete with a T-shirt emblazoned with the word "Coach" (to my eternal pride). How did this experience impact on my own swimming ability? Well, let's just say that what I do in a pool is not so much swim, as not drown. Alas, much like many diligent students of leadership theory, I could simply never translate my brimming theoretical knowledge into effective practice. As Henry Mintzberg, strategy and leadership guru says "Leadership, like swimming, can't be learned by reading about it."[28] I wonder if he knew my story?

Honing your spikiness: purpose, passion and red threads

Purpose – for both individuals and companies – is one of the buzzwords of the moment. And so it should be. Purpose is what keeps us awake at night. It's what gets us out of bed in the morning. It gives life meaning and makes it worth living. Oliver Wendell Holmes laments that "most of us go to our graves with our music still inside us." Purpose is that music – the unique gift we bring to the world.

It's the set of glasses through which we see the world, rather than the glasses through which the world sees us. It is knowing our purpose and the difference we are meant to make in the world that keeps the scourge of imposter syndrome at bay. It is each individual's uniqueness that underpins the benefits of diversity. In the quote below, Theodore Roosevelt talks about the man in the arena who dares greatly again and again, despite the voices of his critics:

It is each individual's uniqueness that underpins the benefits of diversity

It is not the critic who counts; not the man who points out how the strong man stumbles, or where the doer of deeds could have done them better. The credit belongs to the man who is actually in the arena, whose face is marred by dust and sweat and blood; who strives valiantly; who errs, who comes short again and again, because there is no effort without error and shortcoming; but who does actually strive to do the deeds; who knows great enthusiasms, the great devotions; who spends himself in a worthy cause; who at the best knows in the end the triumph of high achievement, and who at the worst, if he fails, at least fails while daring greatly, so that his place shall never be with those cold and timid souls who neither know victory nor defeat.[29]

I love the visual image that this quote conjures up. Purpose is what each of us determine to be our "arena". The place where we need to be brave, keep fighting and dare greatly. And yet

despite its apparent nobility, the arena isn't all peace, joy and fulfilment. It's where we get booed loudly by our critics, where we sweat and trip and stumble, where we fall down and get our nose bloodied. The arena is not for the fainthearted. And yet while it may not be about love, it is about meaning. Because meaning is what keeps us going, meaning is what gets us up for another round even when we feel beaten.

What does your arena look like? What are you striving for? Sweating bullets about? Prepared to throw a punch for? Prepared to bleed for? Prepared to stumble for? Prepared to put yourself out there and be criticised for? What are you putting yourself on the line for? What is your worthy cause?

A few years ago, my arena was something I was vaguely aware of, but not something I could clearly articulate. It came to me, as these things do – gradually, then suddenly as: "To partner with God to help people think differently about their life and their work. To, as a leader, see the angel in the marble and carve until I set it free." (With apologies to Michelangelo!) For me, this means seeing the potential, the unique gifts, in every person or company with whom I interact. It means carving: honing, crafting, creating. It means setting free, letting go so that the angel can fly, reach its potential, be what it is ultimately designed to be!

Doing what you love vs. finding what you love in what you do: the red threads

For many years I believed that if you are propelled by purpose and do what you love, you will "never work another day in your life". And yet despite knowing what gets me up in the morning, being my own boss and having run my own business for the past 15 years, I can't honestly say that I have always soared through each day loving each and every activity.

The truth is, I love most of the things I get to do, but not all of them. And some of them I truly despise. For a long while, feeling like some kind of heretic, I ploughed on – keeping these feelings to myself. Until, feeling drained, demoralised and burnt out I decided to consult a strengths coach for some insight.

What emerged through our conversations and my CliftonStrengths® profile, was the reason why certain activities energised me and others felt like I was watching paint dry. I learned that repetition drains me, whilst working with new ideas, exploring the unknown, maximising what's already great (in people and in companies) and simplifying complexity, energise and stimulate me. It was a scales-from-eyes revelation, no less because through this process I have realised that some of my team love the aspects of our work that drain me and I in turn enjoy those aspects that they do not.

My experience resonated with what Buckingham and Goodall talk about in their book, *Nine Lies about Work.* They describe loving what you do versus finding what you love in what you do as "red threads".[30]

They recount their research with anaesthetists aimed at identifying their red threads. Surprisingly the researchers discovered that despite being equally passionate about their profession, each anaesthetist had completely different and unique red threads. While one truly cherished the opportunity to practise his expertise in getting the human body to hover in exquisite balance between life and death, for another it was all about patient follow-up and restoring people's lives (something that the first guy had zero interest in).

What does this mean for us as leaders? If we acknowledge that as a leader our job is to help those we lead to make meaning for themselves, we need to understand that this web of purpose and strengths is different for everyone, and that it's woven together by each individual's red threads – what he/she uniquely loves about what they do. Indeed, this is one of the superpowers of a Visual Map (which features prominently in part 3) which is a tool and catalyst for this process.

We need to understand that this web of purpose and strengths is different for everyone

Brave enough to show up as yourself: authenticity, vulnerability and emotion

Understanding our purpose helps us to be less concerned about fabricating a persona, playing a role imposed by others, worrying about how other people view us. Purpose liberates us to be authentic. To reveal who we really are. The word "authentic" comes from the Greek word "author" meaning "to write". Are you the author of your story?

Vulnerability is being brave enough to share that story – the "warts and all" version. Rather than being a weakness, vulnerability is the most accurate measure of courage.[31] When we are courageous enough to show our true selves, we risk everything that we most fear: criticism, rejection, not being enough. Despite the presence of "critics", are we brave enough to risk being seen for who we truly are?

Tim Keller's quote about vulnerability, authenticity and love in the context of leadership is profound: "To be loved but not known is comforting but superficial. To be known and not loved is our greatest fear. But to be fully known and truly loved is, well, a lot like being loved by God. It is what we need more than anything. It liberates us from pretence, humbles us out of our self-righteousness, and fortifies us for any difficulty life can throw at us."[32]

Surely, as leaders, this is our challenge: the only way to bring out the best in those we lead, starts with us being brave enough to know ourselves, and brave enough to show up as ourselves.

EQ: the secret sauce

Authenticity is linked to strengths and purpose. It's also linked to emotional intelligence (EQ). EQ and empathy are widely touted as leadership skills for the 21st century.[33]

If as leaders we know what makes us tick (and what makes us angry, frustrated, demoralised, inspired) – it's likely that we will be able to recognise these things in others.

As it turns out, emotions are very important for us to recognise, because while we may prefer to live in a calm, ordered world of rationality, it is actually emotions that influence and drive behaviour! Neuroscientist Antonio Damasio talks about humans as "feeling machines that think".[34]

You will know what I mean if you have experienced the frustration of even the most compelling facts and figures seeming strangely impotent when presented to an audience you aim to influence.

Human beings are meaning-making machines, fuelled by emotional cues. Part of being a leader means understanding how significantly we influence the emotional tone. Leaders are the "feelmakers". A leader's

A leader's feelings, emotions and attitudes are contagious and exert a tremendously powerful effect

feelings, emotions and attitudes are contagious and exert a tremendously powerful effect on those we lead.

Everywhere you go, you always take the "weather" with you!

I remember some years ago having a discussion with my team about the way we were working and how we could improve it. I was stunned when the following pearler emerged: "I know what kind of day I'm going to have by the kind of mood you are in when you walk into the office."

Indeed, I'm not known for emotional stoicism nor my poker face (When Zack was eight years old he used to delight in telling me, "Mommy, I can read you like an Enid Blyton novel!") And yes, there are times when my frustration or irritation with a completely unrelated matter has contaminated my interactions with my team.

Since understanding the effect of my emotions on my team, I've learnt to talk about it as in: "Guys, you might pick up that I'm stressed/irritated/ but it has nothing to do with you or the work we are doing. It's because of XYZ." This works wonders in terms of cleansing the atmosphere. I've realised the powerful influence my emotions have on the culture, and that as a leader I truly "take the weather with me"!

How can we use our emotions to lead?

We spent most of lockdown in 2020 far from the madding crowd, on a farm. It was a haven of much needed serenity. Yet in sharp contrast to my idyllic surroundings, was the crisis that every business in South Africa faced: many of our businesses and those of our clients were hanging on by their fingernails, scrambling to survive.

While the farm oozes tranquillity, it is a little lacking in practicality. We have one big common area (the lodge) which, as it turns out, was the only place where we could access enough Wi-Fi to connect to the outside world. So, while the area was sizeable, it was far from private.

I remember walking in one day to find Bernard, my husband and business partner, on a conference call with his team at MMC, a manganese smelting business that is a continuous operation. Shutdown of any kind is not an option. The previous week the team had moved mountains to put in place an incredible Covid-19 lockdown care and maintenance plan. Their actions were a study in grit, decisiveness and belief… which happen to be their core values. But as we know, last week's miracle inevitably evaporates into today's crisis – and as I entered the lodge, while I couldn't hear the detailed conversation, the fractious tone of the meeting was loud and clear. I scribbled a note to Bernard: "Remember to say thank you," and quickly skedaddled away to mind my own business.

After the call had ended, Bernard thanked me profusely for the simple but timely reminder. After extending his heartfelt appreciation to the team, he could feel how the tone of the meeting changed for the better. His "thank you" set off a cascade of appreciation that went all the way through to the lowest levels, from managers to supervisors, to operators. A reminder of how a simple little "thank you" can turn exhaustion into energy!

A simple little "thank you" can turn exhaustion into energy!

Leading from the heart

During the emotionally charged and uncertain time of Covid-19 I had more conversations about emotions with leaders than ever before. I guess trying to survive a deadly pandemic brings emotions bubbling to the surface. What an amazing opportunity for leaders: to acknowledge that people may be frightened, uncertain, exhausted. To empathise with those feelings and to lead using emotions.

How do leaders do this? By understanding that when people are frightened, they crave kindness. When they are uncertain, they look for reassurance in a plan, and moments of progress towards that plan. And when they are exhausted – they need to be ignited by recognition.

Warren Buffett famously talks about "swimming naked when the tide has gone out" referring to how a crisis lays bare the fault lines underpinning it. Without a doubt, this pandemic has thrown the emotional landscape of the world of work into sharp relief.

This pandemic has thrown the emotional landscape of the world of work into sharp relief

Leaders have realised that a large part of their job involves managing their teams' emotions. Remote working shines a light on trust and autonomy. Do we trust our people to work when we can't actually see them working? In this foreign and emotionally charged environment, small "micro" behaviours have a disproportionate impact: how do we show care and concern for our team members as individuals? How do we encourage them? How do we give them hope when it's in short supply? How do we literally hang in there and hold on when there is very little to hold on to?

Tshepo* is the COO of a large refining business. He contacted me during lockdown and we started having weekly conversations – not about the technicalities of his job, but about his emotional state as a leader of people, and what tools he could use to motivate his team.

We chatted about how difficult it is to give people hope when you yourself just don't know what's going to happen next. This is where the concept of progress really comes into its own. Focusing on the small daily wins (no matter how infinitesimal) energises us and gives us hope to fight another day. It fuels our grander ambitions, and it is essential in times of crisis and uncertainty.

We also talked about how people crave care and attention – and how it's so easy to be permanently firefighting – inevitably resulting in high rates of burnout. Tshepo recalled the time when the entire business had moved mountains to survive the hard lockdown. This involved hundreds of employees camping on-site, living away from their families for five weeks. A tough ask, but it was literally a do or die situation.

The commitment and excitement were palpable, at first, but as time wore on the novelty wore off. Tempers flared. New operational crises presented themselves. Tshepo agreed to institute something called the Hot Seat at the end of each team meeting. This involved going around the table and each person appreciating and recognising their colleague whose turn it was to sit in the "Hot Seat".

According to Tshepo, that was a turnaround moment. It started a cascade of recognition from the boardroom to the plant cellhouse. Suddenly, "thank you" WhatsApp videos were doing the rounds. As a result of this one small change, recognition blossomed, the business was energised, and employees were inspired to go even further to pull miracles out of the bag.

Tshepho and I also talked about vulnerability. The "boss has all the answers" just doesn't cut it – especially in a pandemic. This crisis, like any, is a great equaliser – no one has ever been here before. There are no tried and tested answers. It's a great opportunity for leaders to say, "I don't know, what do you think?" It's a courageous move for a leader, and one that really pays off because it unites the team, and creates psychological safety and trust. As one wise leader I work with put it: "If you are real, you don't always need to be right."

If you are real, you don't always need to be right

We should never underestimate the value of showing our own emotions – what I call the "me too" effect. What this pandemic has done is liberate us to be free to talk about how we are feeling, to reveal who we are when we are at home (including the barking dog, screaming child and hubby in pyjamas who periodically creep into our perfectly curated Zoom backgrounds). It has given us the licence to be vulnerable. To be authentic. To be human!

As leaders it's up to us to tap into this. To use it to connect, to deepen relationships and to truly begin to lead from the heart.

To think about:

- What are your "red threads" – the things that you love about what you do?
- Are you aware of the emotional climate you create? What's been your "weather report" for the past seven days? What do you want your "forecast" to look like?
- Your attitude is contagious – what would people "catch" from yours?
- How often do you have emotional conversations (i.e., not about what work to do, but about how it feels to do the work) with your team?

To do:

Spend time getting to know, understand and articulate your "spikes". Get feedback from your trusted inner circle about the "spikes" they see in you.

Focus on progress (small wins towards the ultimate goal) to address your team's need for certainty in uncertain times.

"In a world where you can be anything, be kind." Ignite your team members' energy by setting aside time to regularly appreciate and recognise them (either in person, or via call or text). Make sure it is specific and highlight what it means to you (this makes your recognition that much more meaningful).

Make a habit of sharing your emotions, both positive and negative, with explanation and context with your team (i.e., "I may appear stressed out today, but it's because our electricity got cut off and I'm feeling a bit overwhelmed – it's nothing to do with you guys!")

Chapter 2: Shut up and listen!

In 2003 Harmony Gold Mining Company acquired AngloGold's Free Gold assets. It was a successful, value accretive transaction, with great assets, not least of whom was firebrand union leader – Thabiso Mofokeng*. Thabiso was a rebel with a cause, renowned for whipping up even the most docile and complacent of workforces into a rabid frenzy. As Free Gold's new owners, Harmony seemed to bring out the worst in him.

After many months of the usual employee relations strategising we, as an executive, were at our wits' end. None of the usual ploys seemed to work with Thabiso, and this was having serious negative ramifications on the transaction as well as the business. As a last resort, Bernard, CEO of Harmony at the time, took my advice and decided to do something a little different: he asked Thabiso for a one-on-one meeting with no agenda. He called it a "listening session".

Thabiso acceded and it was scheduled for one hour on a hot dusty Saturday afternoon, at Thabiso's office in Welkom, some three hundred kilometres away from Bernard's office in Johannesburg.

I drove him there and sat in the car waiting (as sadly there was no Starbucks in which to while away the time). After three hours Bernard emerged, exhausted yet exhilarated. According to him, Thabiso had spent the first hour going through his list of demands (despite their agreement that this session would not be a negotiating session). Then as they both relaxed, Bernard was able to expand the conversation to touch on more personal issues.

As that conversation unfolded, Thabiso shared that the greatest heartache in his life had been when his brother, who worked at Unisel (a Harmony mine) had died in a mine accident. He was deeply hurt by the way that the whole incident was handled by Harmony. It doesn't take a psychologist to understand that this very painful issue was at the root of his animosity towards Harmony.

Bernard could do nothing but listen: he couldn't fix the issue (it had happened many years previously), he couldn't even apologise as it hadn't happened on his watch. And yet, after that conversation, everything shifted. Being listened to had dissipated Thabiso's anger – he became more open, more co-operative and ended up being one of the best union leaders we as a team had the pleasure to work with.

Being listened to had dissipated Thabiso's anger

A world that won't stop talking!

When Zack, our son, was in Grade 1 his school introduced a new reading system (called THRASS). At the time it seemed as if every waking hour went into a THRASS activity of some kind. There was even a rap song, with which Zack proudly entertained us at family gatherings! Similarly, Zack's school education dedicated an enormous amount of time to numeracy in all its forms (Mathletics was a favourite game at the time). Zack also did really well at public speaking. Public "listening"? Not so much, because as we all know there is no such thing.

Great listeners are able to look at the well-known old woman/young woman picture and while clearly seeing either one, accept that someone else may see something different – and acknowledge that both views may be right.[35] Isn't the ability to hold two conflicting ideas in our minds at the same time a fundamental requirement for great leadership? Because to influence, one has to first be influenced. This is the paradox of great listening and I believe, great leadership.

Figure 3: The old woman/young woman illustration[36]

Listening helps you connect

If, as a leader, you want to influence those you lead, you have to form a connection with them. To do this, you have to listen to them. You have to understand their world, and acknowledge the issues they face – their hopes, fears and dreams.

Think about any relationship that you value – there's no doubt that it started with deep, real listening. Listening to another person says: "I value your opinion; I respect you," far more sincerely and eloquently than saying the words themselves.

There are millions of employees in mines, factories, call centres, retail outlets who are dying to be asked, "What do you think?" It's a question I believe could revolutionise our workplaces, transform our cultures and which is the essence of genuine empowerment.

In the words of Henry David Thoreau: "The greatest compliment that was ever paid me was when one asked me what I thought and attended to my answer."[37] Listening is a sign of the greatest respect, and is at the foundation of what all of us really, really want: to be seen, valued and understood.

It might sound like listening takes time and adds complexity, because it means that we can't hold on to black and white views of the world. In reality, because it increases understanding, builds relationships and increases our ability to influence, listening actually SAVES time and increases impact. Consider for a moment Bernard's frustration with Thabiso Mofokeng, the radical union leader. Think about all the time spent (prior to Bernard's listening session) strategising about how to out-manoeuvre him. About how many counter manoeuvres Thabiso managed to marshal in opposition. Yet, as a result of that in-depth listening session, a relationship was formed, and a seed of trust was sown. Not all issues were immediately resolved. But many issues that could have taken years to sort out were progressed.

Listening actually SAVES time and increases impact

Listening blows up stereotypes, and catalyses insights

Some years ago, I was conducting a listening session (i.e., a one-on-one informal chat about the employees' views about the company) with Ben*, a coal miner. Quite awkward at the outset, he gradually relaxed, and when I asked him, "So what keeps you awake at night?" I could see he was genuinely processing his answer.

Often the standard answer to this question revolves around salary, bonus and job security. But this time I was surprised: "I battle every day to get my team of 20 people to do what I need them to do. I think about this all the time but don't know how to do it." (At this point all my senses were humming, because Ben was talking about leadership.)

"So, what do you do now?" I asked. He squirmed a little and said, "Oof, I don't really want to tell you." When I reassured him that our chat was between us and us only, he revealed: "Well, I shout and scream, and often swear at them." When I followed up with: "And how does that work?" he shook his head: "It doesn't." When I asked: "So, what makes you do it?" he said: "Well, that's what my bosses have always done. I know no other way."

Listening to this little story made me understand the power of role modelling – and I realised that it's only when leaders at all levels do things differently on a daily basis, that things will change.

Real listening blows up stereotypes, the neat little boxes that most of us use to simplify a complex world. Stereotypes are filters that prevent us from discerning what's unique about other people. If I had allowed the stereotype that coal miners are only concerned with operational issues to prevail, I may well have missed Ben's insights. But I made a concerted effort to be a good listener – I was genuinely curious about his life, his world and his challenges. And because he sensed that, he opened up to me and shared a valuable nugget about leadership.

That's how listening works a lot of the time – mostly you find what you are not looking for. If I'd asked him, "How would you describe the leadership style here?" would the conversation have unfolded as it did? Not likely!

Okay, so what is listening, really?

At what point, in our schools, universities or workplaces are we ever taught the definition, the value, let alone the skill of listening? I'm not talking about a half-day "listening skills" workshop where you learn how to mirror your colleague, lean forward, purse your lips and knit your brows.

I'm talking about listening as a life skill:

- where we develop the ability to go into another person's world, inhabit it for a brief moment and see it from their point of view;
- where we are able to listen with the intent to deeply understand another human being, emotionally and intellectually.

Listening where we become invisible, where we focus on receiving deep communication from another person's soul, is therapeutic and healing. By giving the other person "oxygen", we meet one of their greatest needs: to be validated and appreciated.

By giving the other person "oxygen", we meet one of their greatest needs: to be validated and appreciated

When people are feeling hurt or misunderstood, and we listen with a pure desire to understand – they will open up.

This kind of listening is the first step to healing pain. This kind of listening has the potential to change the world. For me, it's this kind of listening we need to practise: where we are brave enough to humble ourselves, put aside our own world views, our tightly-held convictions, and our precious ideas – ourselves – and stand in the shoes of another. There's no doubt that this kind of listening should be our first step towards healing the deep-seated hurts of racism, sexism and all kinds of discrimination.

Why is listening so hard?

So, even if at some level, we acknowledge how powerful listening is, it's still really hard to do it. Why is that? Maybe because it's tiring – it takes a huge amount of effort and skill to really listen. And very few people are "listening fit". Perhaps at a deeper level it's because we sense that listening is fundamentally dangerous: when you really immerse yourself in another person's world, you open yourself up to be influenced to see things from their perspective. Real listening requires us to let go of ourselves in the moment, and in this process, we become vulnerable. Herein lies the secret to real connection, that ultimately unlocks our own ability to influence.

How do you become a good listener?

You listen. It's a running family joke that I must have an invisible "I'm listening" sign stamped across my forehead (I have a sizeable forehead, probably big enough to sell advertising space, so it's not impossible to imagine!). Wherever I find myself, be it interacting with a civil servant or a Woolies cashier, people seem keen to open up to me and tell me their stories.

I'm not quite sure why, because I'm a closet introvert, and not much into small talk. But I am curious about other people. Always. So, when the official at the car licensing department opened up to me about his current job and what he dreamed of doing one day, I was fascinated. I wanted to hear more. I asked questions. (The people in the queue behind me were simmering, but I only noticed afterwards). Same with the Woolies cashier: as I unpacked my groceries she told me about her background, her family struggles and her hopes and dreams.

Similarly, in a corporate setting, listening sessions are high up on my list of favourite activities. I conducted my fair share of listening sessions during my Harmony days, and I acknowledge that it's much easier to listen when you are an external consultant. The natural defensiveness and need to correct "wrong" assumptions simply aren't there. I love that in one hour we can reach a level of intimacy in our discussion that can have people brought to tears or banging on the table in frustration or passion.

But, but, but… when I'm not in listening mode, I tend to be a serial interrupter (ask my family and close work colleagues). I often can't quell my excitement at immediately inserting my new idea into the conversation (usually before the other person has finished talking about their idea). And then there's my tendency to interrupt most poor souls who attempt to tell me a story. I'm obsessed by often irrelevant details that help complete the Netflix mini-movie taking shape in my head (Where did you meet? What was she wearing?), which understandably seriously peeves the storyteller.

A mindset of "compulsive curiosity about discovering the poetry and wisdom that is within people"

Listening requires skill and will, but at its core it is about a mindset of "compulsive curiosity about discovering the poetry and wisdom that is within people" (to paraphrase Kate Murphy.)[38] You can't fake it. You can't go through the motions. You need to be genuinely fascinated by the unpredictable utterings that come out of people's mouths.

One life-changing discovery that has helped me enormously is Nancy Kline's *Time to Think* material.[39] Bernard and I trained in the Thinking Partners methodology eight years ago and still apply it to this day.

Essentially, it involves one partner inhabiting the role of the Thinker, and the other the role of the Listener. The Listener asks the Thinker one question: "What is it that you would like to think about, and what are your thoughts so far?" What makes this a game changer are the rules: The Listener is not allowed to interrupt AT ALL, except to ask, "What more?"

There's NO adding to the Thinker's train of thought with your own brilliant insights and ideas. No comments, critiques, or judgements. The Thinker has the freedom to think out loud in a safe place without the fear of being interrupted.

For the Thinker, this feels a little bit like standing on the top of Table Mountain with the world at your feet: there's no pressure to sound coherent, to think insightfully, to even think in full sentences (who does that anyway?). The results are phenomenal as my story below demonstrates.

A few years ago, Bernard and I were away for a weekend and went for our regular run. Running is usually when we do our Thinking Partners exercise. This time it was Bernard's turn to be the Thinker. He wanted to think out loud about a specific board position that he had been offered. I knew about this and had some strong opinions about it.

I almost bombed the whole Thinking Partners exercise in favour of a "proper" discussion (i.e., where I could voice my strongly-held views). But I was too late. Bernard had already begun thinking aloud, as is the Thinker's right.

As we jogged along and I huffed and puffed, Bernard laid out the issue with all its pros and cons. My breathlessness probably saved the day here because although I had a great need to chime in and add my thoughts on multiple occasions, I simply didn't have enough air! I was basically reduced to "all ears" and "no words". (Perhaps that's one of the reasons this Thinking Partners method works so well on our runs?!).

After an hour, Bernard had thought aloud about all the issues and most of his thoughts echoed my own. As we cooled down he said: "Wow. That was great, it really helped. Thanks so much. I'll go and send the email right now." I was aghast! I had a sudden sliding doors* moment: had we engaged in a normal conversation, this would definitely have gone horribly wrong. I would not have held back on my (mostly) negative opinions. Bernard would have felt the need to counter my views. We would have argued. Not a chance would we have ended up with him agreeing to send an email that mirrored my own thoughts about the situation.

Some skills

For all of us, the struggle is real, but if you have the mindset and the will to listen, there are some basic skills that I have found to be very useful.

1. Work on your supportive responses

Have you ever been in a conversation where you share something personal, such as, "I felt really sick over the weekend, I thought I was coming down with something" and the response is: "Really? Actually, this weekend I was really ill, what a drama." This is known as a shift response. The "listener" is shifting the focus of the conversation to themselves. This is the opposite of a supportive response, whereby the speaker feels truly listened to: "Oh wow, what happened? How did you deal with it? Do you feel any better now?" As a leader, if you want people to open up, feel seen, recognised and listened to, you need to practise your supportive responses.

2. Put away your phone

There's also really basic stuff like putting away your cell phone. Simon Sinek talks about how even the presence of a cell phone (face down) on a table heightens people's anxiety

* *Sliding Doors is a movie about alternative realities playing out.*

about being interrupted.[40] Think about the message it sends: "you are important, but not as important as a call which I may need to take". Another practical tip is to discourage passage conversations in favour of a proper sit-down. This sends the signal that the person is important and worthy enough of your undivided attention.

3. Look 'em in the eyes? Or not

There is some compelling research about face-to-face eye contact increasing intimacy and enhancing listening, and there are many instances where it does just that.[41] Having said that, though, I've probably had more intimate conversations in cars, on planes and jogging where we were both facing the same direction and no eye contact was possible. Perhaps it's the lack of eye contact that makes people more relaxed about expressing their deepest thoughts?

4. Ask the right questions, and wait

This is a quality rather than quantity game. Peppering people with questions that make them feel like they are being interrogated is not helpful. Great listeners are calm, patient and comfortable with silence – something that's quite unusual in our babbling, self-promoting society. It's notable that LISTEN is a perfect anagram of SILENT! Sometimes we don't want to listen because we are afraid of not knowing what to say in response. In our "I always know all the answers" culture, it's refreshingly genuine to say: "I don't know, what do you think?" or even "I'm not sure, let me think about that." Nothing will make a person feel more respected or valued than when you pick up a conversation with "I've been thinking about what you said."

LISTEN is a perfect anagram of SILENT!

Finally: A not-so-fringe benefit

Listening is powerful, not just because it enables the listener to leave with a better understanding of their counterpart's world, but also because the process of thinking out loud empowers the thinker to untangle his/her thoughts, evaluate decisions, own them and ultimately implement them.

To think about:

- Ask yourself…who listens to you? Who do you listen to?
- Are you a good listener? When? To whom?
- Who/what are you curious about?

To do:

Schedule regular "listening sessions" with colleagues and direct reports.

Find out something interesting about a colleague/teammate, and share something that not many people know about you.

Here's a list of conversation starters/positively framed questions to use with family, friends and teammates:

Work focused:

- What's been your best moment working in this company?
- What keeps you awake at night?
- Tell me about a time you were really happy at work? What happened?
- Tell me about a time you were really frustrated with the work you do? What happened?
- What three things would you change if you became CEO tomorrow?

- What are your three wishes for this company?
- What gets you out of bed in the morning?

Person focused:

- If you could invite anyone in the world to dinner, who would it be?
- What does your perfect day look like?
- When did you last sing to yourself?
- What's the best compliment anyone has ever paid you?
- For what in your life do you feel most grateful?
- If you could wake up tomorrow having gained one skill/ability what would it be?
- What is something that you have always dreamed about doing?
- What is the greatest accomplishment of your life?
- What do you value most in a friendship?
- What's your most treasured memory?

Chapter 3: Connect using the power of stories

About six months after I resigned from Harmony (in 2007) I received a call from one of our renowned business schools requesting me to lecture their executive MBA class on strategy execution. I was ecstatic: here was my chance to share my learning and experience with people that would be able to use it.

The business school was clear about one thing though, don't include anything personal: "Just the facts, Ma'am." Everything had to be factual and replicable. Not knowing then what I know now, I was happy to acquiesce: "No problem." Little did I realise the havoc that those two little words would wreak.

Half an hour into my eight-hour session, the audience, disengaged from the outset, seemed to be deteriorating. What could be wrong? I sought refuge in my slides (I had many!) Surely somewhere a slide or concept would connect with them? Sadly, that never happened. The day just got progressively worse (I remember wondering whether running away from a business school was an option?). I died a thousand deaths that day. Only many years later, when I encountered Anecdote's *Storytelling for Leaders* programme, did I realise my big mistake that fateful day: I was one hundred slides too heavy and one hundred stories too light.

As part of processing this traumatic experience, I told myself that lecturing, presenting or any form of public speaking was simply not for me. Writing was my medium of communication with the world. And so, in 2016 I wrote a book.

One unforeseen snag is that when you write a book (which you would like people to read) you need to talk about it! In public! To large groups of people! See the problem? I'm not sure what I would have done in the absence of meeting Shawn Callahan and Mark Schenk from Anecdote (the largest business storytelling firm globally), and working with them to learn about how to use the power of story.

In 2016 Bernard and I were trained and accredited to deliver their *Storytelling for Leaders* programme and are currently the only accredited Anecdote partners on the African continent.

I'll never forget doing a talk about my book in early 2017 to an audience of close to a thousand people: my hands were sweaty, my heart racing. But I started with a story – and it worked! The audience smiled, sat forward and engaged. Taking them with me on an intellectual journey about the dismal state of leadership and what we needed to do about it was smooth sailing from there on. And as for that "I'm not a public speaker" story that I had told myself – I replaced it with a new story: to connect with an audience and make my message stick, I need to be brave enough to tell stories. And not just any stories – my stories!

To connect with an audience and make my message stick, I need to be brave enough to tell stories

For me the power of storytelling as a tool of connection, influence and leadership is not merely intellectual but deeply personal: I can vouch for it because I have seen it, felt it and experienced it!

What kind of stories?

Personally, I love the word "story." Unfortunately though in many people's minds it's a word that conjures up fairy tales, Harry Potter, the hero's journey, even Luke Skywalker! Anecdote refers to this as "Big S storytelling". The good news is that unless you want to work for Disney or Pixar, Big S skills are not required. As leaders we are not required to create epic narratives. Quite the contrary. In fact, examples of everyday events, that are concrete, relatable and affect us on an emotional level, are far more useful.

The story I shared (in part one) about my encounter with Jabulani, the security guard that embodied the value of integrity in a such tangible way is a "little s" story: it's concrete, specific and memorable. There are a million of these little moments happening in our workplaces all day, every day. These are the stories that not only give our lives meaning and colour, but also form the fabric of the corporate culture. We need to identify them, capture them and remember to retell them.

Five reasons why stories make your message stick!

Much like my dire lecturing experience, most leaders' infatuation with complex, abstract jargon presented on PowerPoint slides hinders rather than helps their communication effort – despite their best intentions. Stories cut through clutter, are easy to recall and create connection, enhancing leaders' chances to get their messages to stick. Here are five reasons why stories work so well.

#1. Stories are memorable and impactful

Stories make things concrete. They allow us to see and conjure up a time, a place, characters, events, dialogue and an outcome in our mind's eye. They solve for the abstract.

Stories also make us feel something: hopeful, sad, frustrated, optimistic. It's these emotions that etch stories on our hearts, making them memorable and impactful. Deluged as we are in an increasingly cluttered world, the emotions inherent to stories make them stand out.

A few years ago, at our Joburg Indaba Conference, Bernard, in his role as chairman, needed to introduce Mark Cutifani, the CEO of Anglo American, who had flown out from London for the keynote presentation. Rather than read out Mark's pre-approved, substantial and impressive CV, Bernard told a story (much to the consternation of Mark's PR team).

He recounted the night we were invited to the Cutifani residence in a leafy suburb of Johannesburg for a casual braai. As we sat around chatting over pre-braai drinks, we noticed Mark and his wife, Luanna exchange a secret signal. Without a word, Luanna got up, walked over to the braai and proceeded to braai every last piece of meat (to perfection!) It was delicious and as Bernard said by means of introduction, "Not only are you my favourite Aussie, but you are the only guy I know who gets his wife to braai!"

That night over cocktails guess what people were talking about? Mark's very comprehensive PowerPoint presentation? Or the anecdote about his wife doing the braaiing?

Facts are important but stories are like a clothes hanger: they give the facts, shape, meaning and context. Do you remember the facts and figures around David and Goliath, Little Red Riding

Hood, Romeo and Juliet? No? But I bet you could tell the story pretty accurately! According to research conducted by two Stanford professors, Gordon Bower and Michal Clark, we are six to seven times more likely to remember a story than a set of facts.[42] This means that as a leader you are giving your message a 600% better chance of being recalled if you wrap it in a story. Definitely worth it at those odds, I believe!

We are six to seven times more likely to remember a story than a set of facts

#2. Stories convey emotions and emotions inspire action

People (friends, colleagues, employees) go to war for stories. Why? Because stories make us feel something. Passionate. Excited. Fearless. Exactly the stuff we always say we want people to feel about the business.

Stories refresh and energise us. They inspire us to action. Here is a classic anecdote that occurred during the Harmony/Goldfields hostile bid some years ago. Two erstwhile friends (from each of the rival companies) gathered for their customary Saturday evening braai. Talk inevitably turned to the bid. Figures about productivity, efficiency, innovation were effortlessly cited. But despite the facts, each friend stuck steadfastly to his "story". Passions rose. Punches flew! And the Monday-morning-black-eye was sheepishly attributed to "taking one for the Harmony story"!

#3. Stories create our identity, our culture, and colour our destiny

Stories breathe life into abstract concepts like strategy, culture, and values. Who understands exactly what is meant by "integrity" except through a concrete anecdote or example of someone in the business actually living it through his/her actions? Analogies (which are micro-stories) work in a similar way. As leaders, instead of talking about strategic intent or vision, we need to paint a picture of the "Everest" we dream of summiting, or the "Comrades Marathon" we aim to complete.

Stories are powerful forces in communicating identity to the outside world. Brands ("short stories" as opposed to "epic novels") have long been proved to be assets on companies' balance sheets. Hard-nosed investors and fund managers, while rigorously analysing the facts, often can find no other reason than a "good story" for an unexplained valuation gap.

Purpose, a popular idea of the moment is integrally intertwined with story. What do we tell ourselves about who we are and what we want to become? What is the story of our future? Are we "survivors"? Do we want to challenge the status quo? Create a better world? A strong narrative brings people together, creates a cohesive sense of identity and amplifies events. In the same way, a weak or non-existent story or narrative diminishes our experience.

When the South African national rugby team (the Springboks) won the Rugby World Cup in 1995, after being re-admitted to the competition due to the end of apartheid, it was a country-making event. Did the subsequent 2007 World Cup win feel the same? For many, by then the hope and magic of the Miracle Rainbow Nation narrative had substantially waned, diminishing the overall effect.

#4. Stories instantly convey authenticity, vulnerability and create connection

Sharing personal stories enables leaders to reveal that they too are human beings. Stories help convey authenticity and vulnerability, which help leaders connect with employees. Followers' craving to know more about their leaders is not satisfied by the trite reeling off of an impressive CV. They want a "show, don't tell" insight into who their leader is, because character can never be demonstrated by facts.

And in return, the opportunity to share their own story is deeply appreciated. When we "speak story" we unearth insights about others, discover common experiences and for a moment are able to see life from the other person's point of view. Empathy blossoms.

The shortest distance between two people is a story.

We see daily evidence in the work that we do as THINKspiration – be it at the most senior levels or at the shopfloor or rockface – that indeed the shortest distance between two people is a story.

#5. Stories are influence tools that change people's minds

The facts and fiction surrounding Covid-19 misinformation continue to demonstrate a "power of story" mantra that "you can't change people's minds with the facts, only with a better story". Why? Because all of us, when presented with a set of facts that challenge our existing beliefs, are triggered. More specifically our confirmation bias is triggered.

This means that rather than listening to and processing information contrary to our existing beliefs, we immediately raise our defences, screen out the dissenting information and push back hard, looking for new or alternative facts to reconfirm our existing beliefs.

Stories, however, work differently: because they draw us in, and pull us toward them rather than pushing against our existing beliefs – they don't trigger confirmation bias and our defences. Stories work by stealth, driven by the neural coupling or mirroring that takes place between the brainwaves of the storyteller and the brainwaves of the story listener, making the listener open and receptive to new information.

Story-powered leadership

So, the arguments above are compelling, right? But maybe you just don't see yourself as a storyteller. Mostly, when we ask leaders, "Who thinks of themselves as a storyteller?" one or two at most raise their hands. And yet this contrasts sharply with the evidence from the work of evolutionary biologist Robin Dunbar.

He assigned graduate students to eavesdrop on people's conversations, in restaurants, coffee shops, and on public transport (what an assignment, just saying!). His research proved that more than 60% of the time people are having conversations about people saying and doing things – in other words, telling each other stories.[43]

We all speak story

According to scientists, "story" is our native language.[44] It's hard-wired into our brains from babyhood. Kids from as young as two respond to stories and make up their own as a way of making sense of their surroundings. But as we get older, fairy tales and fiction are relegated in favour of real world

"story" is our native language

facts and figures. I'm not against facts, but they simply do not (as we often repeat) "speak for themselves". To really stick, facts need to be "wrapped in context and emotion" – which happens to be our official definition of story (courtesy of Anecdote).

So, our innate story-ability exists, even if for some of us it's more dormant than others. How do we re-awaken it, reconnect with it, and use it to lead? And how do we unleash its power in a business context?

Recognise that we are doing it anyway

In 1944 Heider and Simmel conducted research that proved that humans are meaning-making machines: after showing subjects a silent two-minute video of a series of geometric shapes (circles, squares and triangles) moving around on a screen, they asked them to describe what they had just observed.

Out of thirty-five respondents, thirty-four used stories varying from bullying, to domestic violence, to divorce, to world war-type scenarios to explain what was happening. The odd one out talked about seeing three geometric shapes moving across a two-dimensional plane (clearly an engineer!).[45]

We do this all the time: think about your reaction when you arrive at work and see the CEO's car parked out front, a clear signal of business UNusual. What runs through your mind? In the context of a global pandemic, probably nothing good! Does this mean we have a positive case? Or is the CEO here to talk about retrenchments? Yes! That's probably it!

Later, when you walk past the corporate communication boardroom and see the CEO and the communication team together, perhaps you remember that it's preparation time for the quarterly results, and travel restrictions preventing group travel would explain why the CEO has come to them instead.

Do you notice what happened here? Based on a few abstract facts – the CEO's presence (unusual); the context (Covid-19; business pressure) fears (positive Covid-19 cases, retrenchments) = a disaster story! Then, as result of more information (the CEO sitting with the communication team; a belated realisation – they can't travel, and quarterly results are coming up) = bingo – an alternative to the disaster story! Just like Heider and Simmel's subjects constructed stories about the geometric shapes in the video, we all make sense of disconnected events by constructing our own stories about them.

We tell ourselves stories all the time to "fill in the gaps". Why did my friend not respond to my WhatsApp message? Perhaps she is annoyed at a remark that I made which I meant as a joke? What about my boss who arrived late and looks like a thundercloud about to erupt? Could it be that she is disappointed with our performance as a team?

Of course, it's very likely that my friend is hectically busy dealing with a work crisis, and that my boss arrived in a tizz after dealing with her tantrummy teenager who had an ill-timed meltdown. But in the absence of knowing the actual story, I have filled in the blanks with a different story, and that's the story I'm telling myself right now.

Telling ourselves stories helps us to make sense of incoming information – but these stories may be inaccurate or outright damaging. As leaders we need to be aware of these stories and actively help those we lead to surface "the story I'm telling myself" (which is how Brené Brown refers to it) as a way of clarifying and often correcting hidden assumptions, as per the story I eventually unearthed – that I was no good as a public speaker – after my rather disastrous lecturing endeavour.[46]

What is a story?

One of the best things about Anecdote's storytelling expertise is its frameworks. For the more technically minded among us, these "recipes" transform storytelling from an art into a craft, which like any skill can be learnt and practised. The Anecdote "What is a story?" framework is simple yet powerful. The framework specifies five characteristics:

1. Time/place marker
2. Series of events
3. Dialogue
4. Outcome (often unexpected)
5. Business point[47]

The time and/or place marker

This makes the story concrete. You may be asking yourself about the relevance of my mentioning (a few pages ago) that the Cutifani's house was in a leafy suburb of Johannesburg. How does that make any difference? It does, though, because it functions as a trigger to the listener to start their version of the movie. By encouraging the listener to picture a location (even if it's imaginary) – the story and all the information it contains becomes concrete.

I've realised that I crave this concrete detail in other people's anecdotes. When Bernard starts telling me about his day and mentions his coffee with a colleague, I cannot help but interrupt, asking, "Where?" (I'm not proud of this, and it is a constant source of irritation for him). To his answer of, "Tasha's," I will definitely follow up with: "Nicolway? Melrose? Morningside?" (It's not my fault that it's a franchise!). I've learnt that unless I have this crucial bit of information, I can't process the rest of the conversation – the camera in my mind's eye simply will not roll.

The series of events

This is the: "What happened?" moment. As demonstrated in my integrity story (in part 1) involving the security guard Jabulani: "I went through the turnstile, I had lots of bags, I (unknowingly) dropped my wallet, I completed my presentation and departed via the security turnstile."

Dialogue

This is otherwise known as the "he said/she said" moment. Most of our conversations in a social setting are filled with these moments. Dialogue is a powerful conduit of emotion. My Jabulani security guard story could have been improved if I had recounted more details about the actual conversation, as in: "Oh my goodness Jabulani, that's incredible. I didn't even realise I had dropped it. Thank you, you have made my day."

The unexpected outcome

This is the element of surprise, the plot twist. In the story above this would be the "I didn't even realise I had dropped it" moment. In addition to enhancing the impact and memorability of the story, it hooks the listener in, and is their incentive to keep listening. Will they learn something? Find out something they didn't know? See an issue a little differently?

The business point

Every story must have a business point, or why are you telling it? This does not mean that the only stories you tell are business stories. I find that most of the stories I tell originate outside of business but have a business point.

In the Jabulani story the business point is simply about a value in action – "that's integrity". This story has demonstrated an abstract value in a very concrete way. The business point can also be used to preface the story, as in: "I saw an incredible example of integrity in action last year when I visited…" (continue with the story as above). Finish with, "Now that's integrity."

Putting stories to work – some health warnings

As simple and easy as it is to put stories to work, there are some do's and don'ts, courtesy of Anecdote, as well as borne out by my own experiences. Here they are:

Don't use the S word

As much as I personally love the word "story", I've come to accept that I'm the exception. For most people if you preface what you are about to say with, "Let me tell you a story…" they groan inwardly, expecting a long, irrelevant yarn, a fairy-tale or possibly even something patronising.

Why give yourself a disadvantage from the get-go? Rather go straight into the story, or preface it with, "Let me share an example that shows… (insert business point)."

Don't overexplain the business point

Think of the business point as the punchline of a joke. There's nothing worse than a raconteur desperately telling you why his joke is funny. It's the same with the business point: resist the temptation to gabble on.

Keep them short – don't include irrelevant detail

Oral stories need to be short, snappy and succinct. As a general rule, no longer than ninety seconds. This requires the discipline not to ramble and the skill to weed out non-essential details, while retaining key parts of the story that make it work.

Written stories can be a little longer due to the slightly longer attention span of the average reader. It's important to include enough detail to trigger the mini-Netflix moment but to stop short of overwhelming the audience.

Keep them fresh

As captivating as stories are, no one wants to be known as a one-story wonder. I recall a colleague I worked with many years ago, who worked his story about growing up as a shepherd boy in rural South Africa into every meeting. Charmed by the story the first time, by what felt like the hundredth time, the eye rolling was real.

Make them relevant

Thinking about which stories are relevant to which audiences requires preparation and time and is undoubtedly worth the effort. Using the power of story to connect with a group of business leaders requires a different "connection" story to conducting a workshop with school teachers.

Stories at work: some examples

Putting Stories to Work is the title of our Anecdote partner, Shawn Callahan's book.[48] It's a fabulous and worthwhile read, not least because Shawn actually shows us how to make stories work in a business setting.

It's liberating to discover that the stories we use in business don't have to be stories about business. But what is critical is that we tell relevant stories and seamlessly link them to a well thought through business point.

The best way of illustrating this is by sharing an example (I almost wrote "story"!) with you. In early 2017, I got a call requesting me to talk to a church group about leadership. Thinking about my message, I landed on three takeaways or leadership lessons that I wanted to share:

Lesson 1: Leaders' words have disproportionate impact: what you say has far more impact than you could ever imagine.

Lesson 2: You can never see your own blind spots – insights from a trusted team are incredibly valuable and can prevent disaster.

Lesson 3: Incentives don't always work like you think they will. Be careful which behaviour you want to incentivise – you will get exactly that.

Now allow me to walk you through two scenarios: the "no story" approach and the "power of story" approach.

The "no story" approach

I go to some trouble to prepare a dazzling PowerPoint presentation. It contains an expanded version of my key points: lots of bullet points, complete with some impressive graphics and facts and figures. I know I have a lot of slides and tons of information, and I hope I have enough time to get through all my slides. There's unlikely to be time for questions, but that's what they want, right?

Can you see a repeat performance of my Business School horror movie lining up?

The "power of story" approach

Although I have my three leadership lessons in mind, I start by thinking about the audience and the best way to connect with them. The audience is a diverse mix of age, income and education level, making a targeted connection story challenging. I need to choose stories that make my points and that are also relatable across the board. I decide on one PowerPoint slide (see I'm not completely anti-PowerPoint!) with minimal copy and three photos as seen below:

Figure 4: Three leadership lessons. Source: THINKspiration

After a brief introduction, I share the following three stories clearly re-iterating the business points.

Lesson 1:

Business point: Words matter. What leaders say has impact and far-reaching consequences. Life (or death) is in the power of a leader's tongue.

Story: I very clearly remember the day Mrs James, my Grade 2 teacher, called me up to the front of the class and told me that she wanted to take me to the principal's office. Being rather keen to avoid conflict and be a good girl, this did not immediately strike me as great news. But Mrs James quickly reassured me: "Don't worry, my dear, it's nothing bad, I just want to show him your creative writing… which I think deserves a 'good work stamp'." Still, I was reluctant. The principal, Mr Sounes, was a rather formidable figure – ancient, unsmiling and shrouded by cigar smoke. Definitely to be avoided at all costs. But before I knew it, Mrs James had my hand in hers and there we were in the principal's office. But I was in luck – Mr Sounes wasn't available that day. So instead we got to visit the much younger, more approachable and charming Vice Principal, Mr De Klerk. He smiled a lot and clearly didn't smoke. But more than that his words left an indelible imprint on me – one that I held on to for many years after our meeting (particularly when I doubted myself): "Wow, Tracey, this is great. You never know, maybe you will be a writer someday!"

Lesson 2:

Business point: You can never see your own blind spots

Story: I grew up with the Famous Five. Despite Enid Blyton's classist, sexist, and racist undertones that are glaringly obvious to me now – as a child, desperate to be part of the gang, they sailed over my eight-year-old head.

What a joy then, by chance to have created our own THINKspiration version of the Famous Five. Lisa, Dalu, Siviwe, Wezo, and I adopted the moniker during an extended road trip last year and it stuck. Like our namesakes, we go on adventures and uncover interesting insights, brainstorm solutions – and have an absolute ball while doing it.

Mostly, our destinations are not glamorous and not usually anywhere we can easily fly to – so it's road trips all the way. And since I have access to the biggest car (Bernard's Prado) I'm usually in the driver's seat. The journeys are long, and the roads are tricky – you are always between a pothole, an ore truck and an oncoming vehicle. But the other four keep me sane: whether it's Lisa telling me that yes, according to Waze AND Google maps AND the official directions – we are on the right road or Siv (after some loud praying) congratulating me on a rather adrenaline-inducing overtake ("I love how calm and decisive you were, Tracey!")

After one particularly gruelling journey, we finally arrived at our accommodations. Nothing fancy – little, round huts with the atmospheric sound of an ore crusher in the background. Buoyed by having survived the trip, we all hopped in the car for our drive to dinner. I thought the worst was behind me – and it almost was! Literally!

As I reversed out of the parking space, the four yelled as one: STOOOOOP! I did: stopping half a millimetre away from a huge tree that had been in my blind spot! Thanks to my team, disaster had been averted. Safe to say that we all had a big glass of wine that night, and raised our glasses to "a team that helps you to see your blind spots"!

Lesson 3:

Business point: Be careful which behaviour you want to incentivise – you will get exactly that

Story: When Zack was in Grade 2, his well-intentioned teacher implemented a reading incentive programme. It worked like this: if Zack completed ten minutes of reading a day, he could colour in an apple in his reading tree and once all the apples were coloured in, Zack would get a reward. At the time, Zack loved reading and it consumed most of his free time, as he was already reading way beyond the stipulated ten minutes. Enter the reading incentive programme: Zack faithfully did his ten minutes a day – but no more, proudly declaring: "But Mommy, why do I have to read for longer, I have done my ten minutes!"

These stories only take a few minutes to relay, but while I'm sharing them I can see people's eyes lighting up; they are sitting forward, engaging – this is what connection looks like. When I'm done there's ample time for comments and questions, and that's a good thing because there are a lot.

The rest of the session is a conversation – in which everyone feels free to participate with their own stories – rather than a presentation. Eighteen months later I am delighted by a connection request on LinkedIn. It's from someone who was in the audience that day, who specifically referred to my stories, all those months ago! Proof indeed that stories make our messages stick!

Story listening

The foundation of storytelling is story listening. Listening to others' stories is as valuable in creating connections with people as sharing your stories with them. All the arguments for and provisos about the power of listening in the previous chapter apply.

The foundation of storytelling is story listening

Adding the power of story to the value of listening results in exponential benefits. Often, when listening we try to dig underneath generalities, opinions and trite abstractions to unearth meaningful insights. This is when encouraging your audience to share a real life example, which invariably leads to a story, is enlightening. Story listening catalyses aha moments (both in the teller and the listener) and in this way provides an insightful and accurate barometer of corporate culture.

But people won't just share their stories because you ask them to. To get people to open up about experiences which are meaningful to them – you need to create the right conditions:

Share your intent: Stories expose people and they will need to feel psychologically safe by understanding why you want to know and how their stories will be used. Make sure you have their permission to retell their stories if appropriate.

Show genuine interest: Listening is about far more than the active listening signals many of us have been taught over the years. So, no amount of pursing your lips, echoing the salient points, knitting your brows and leaning forward will be a substitute for genuine desire to, for a moment, inhabit someone else's world. Interest borne of genuine curiosity simply can't be faked.

Create an informal "environment": While sharing a glass of wine or bonding over a delicious cappuccino is more conducive to story sharing, that isn't always possible or practical. At THINKspiration when we conduct listening sessions in which we collect stories, we often face challenging conditions: as interviewers we are aware that we are an imposition squeezed in to a complete stranger's diary for reasons often unclear to them.

My team and I lean on our experience to quickly create rapport and a sense of trust. I think that genuine curiosity does the trick. Once people realise that you are listening intently to them, they relax and open up. In almost every case people leave the session thanking us for our time and sharing how much they enjoyed it.

Tell your own stories: Many times, driving home after school with Zack I've asked the, "How was your day?" question, hoping that it would uncover a groundswell of anecdotes resulting in genuine understanding and insights about his school life and experience. Sadly, it never has. His monosyllabic "good" or "fine" retort takes blandness to a new level.

Following it up with, "What made it good?" or even, "Tell me more," is just another brick wall. But if I start sharing the stories of my day as in: "I had such a stressful meeting today, the IT didn't work, so I had to make it up as I went along" or, "We got so lost going to a client… " – the "That's nothing" effect kicks in. It's what happens when everyone is chatting around a braai or dinner and someone shares their disastrous airline story, and then someone else says, "Hey – that's nothing… " and shares their even more disastrous airline story, and so it continues. I've found that sharing my own stories and anecdotes is one of the best ways of eliciting stories from others.

There is a knack to this, though, and here are some tricks of the trade that I use all the time (courtesy of Anecdote) :

- Never say, "Tell me a story…" The S word again works at cross purposes here. What happens in the listener's mind is a kind of brain-freeze – a panicky blank combined with thoughts about: "Oh no, I don't know any stories, I can't tell stories, I'm useless at storytelling… Oh no, I can't do this." This internal dialogue is neatly encapsulated in a blank stare, and most often the verbal response is: "I can't think of one right now."
- What works far better is to ask the listener to share a moment, a time, or an example and link this to an emotion: i.e., "Tell me about a moment when you felt really frustrated in this job?" If you follow this up with, "What happened?" a story is bound to follow.
- The best story triggering questions are, "What happened?", "When?" and "Where?" because they take us to a time, a place and events /activities.
- Avoid the "Why?" question at all costs. This is tough for me, as it is my favourite question, but I've seen over and over that if you ask why, you end up with an opinion, a generalisation, an assertion – but not a story.

To think about:

- Hone your story spotting antennae, by looking out for the key characteristics that define a story.
- How could you link personal stories to relevant business points you would like to make?
- Where could you find or source stories to use as examples?
- Before a meeting or presentation, how could you use a relevant story to connect with your audience?

To do:

What system could you use to build up a database of stories, which you can access as you need to?

Make a note of the power of "what happened" as a story eliciting question as in:

- Think back over the past few weeks about a time when you got to the end of the day and thought "I've had a great day." What happened?
- Or think about a low point, a time when you thought "I hate this job." What happened?

PART THREE

Leading Others

"Of the best leaders they will say, we did it ourselves."

– Chinese proverb

Can you imagine your strategy* as a compelling visual story which is owned, discussed and effectively implemented on a daily basis by all employees?

Do you believe this is possible?

If so, read on for the four simple steps that you can take to make it happen!

Step 1: Paint a picture of the future you want to create

Step 2: Listen to where your people are

Step 3: Distil your strategy into a compelling story and visualise it

Step 4: Empower all your employees – from the boardroom to the shopfloor – to tell it from their perspective

---

* *A complex web of initiatives regarding future direction of the business, purpose, vision and mission, operating practices, desired culture, values, leadership style and plans to achieve these.*

Chapter 4: Paint a picture of the future you want to create

I love "the future". It's a place where imagination triumphs over the messy reality we have to untangle on a daily basis. It's also a powerful beacon of hope – enticing and encouraging. "The future" means that we have something to get out of bed for. Something to work for. Something to make happen or die trying. It's every business's magnetic force. It energises, inspires, takes us forward.

It is said that the best way to predict the future is to invent it. Inventing requires visualising, imagining and using that perspective to guide your actions and decisions in the present moment. Visualising something allows you to literally see it twice: first in your imagination, and the second time in reality. World class athletes often visualise the perfect shot, the perfect serve – the perfect victory! Visualising the future that you want to create as a leader has a similar effect.

Visualising something allows you to literally see it twice: first in your imagination, and the second time in reality.

As I mentioned in my introduction, at the age of ten, my big dream was to win Wimbledon. I never did, but I did end up with a tennis scholarship in the US. Tennis taught me a lot – most of all that to chase a dream, you have to visualise it so clearly that you can make decisions "today" based on the future that you want to create.

My initial Wimbledon dream, which was later replaced by my more realistic US scholarship dream was a fire that burned in my heart every single day. It inspired me to wake up every morning at five to practice my forehand and second serve (which always needed a little extra), to sit every Sunday night and call my list of practice partners to arrange that week's sessions, to jump rope every day for ten continuous minutes.

I clearly remember those times when it was hard or when I was tired, playing badly, in a slump or had suffered a bad loss, that it was my dream that kept me going.

Why a picture of the future works

In the words of Antoine de St Exupery: "If you want to build a ship, don't drum up the men to gather wood, divide the work, and give orders. Instead, teach them to yearn for the vast and endless sea."[49]

For both companies and individuals there's an enormous benefit in having painted their picture of the future or having articulated their version of a much yearned for "vast and endless sea". Why? Because everyone fears the unknown. It's part of the human condition.

> Followers seek out leaders who are able to paint a compelling and vivid picture of the future.

Followers seek out leaders who can alleviate this unconscious fear – leaders who are able to paint a compelling and vivid picture of the future. This works at an emotional level because it enables leaders to transform people's often-unexpressed fear and anxiety into something far more positive: hope, inspiration, excitement, the thrill of an adventure. By creating confidence in an as yet unconstructed future, leaders provide an antidote to uncertainty, and become dealers in hope.

Painting a picture of the future works on a practical, rational level too: because the leader and his/her team can literally "time-travel", and stand in their imagined future. It enables them to take today's decisions with the benefit of hindsight.

Every day, leaders make decisions about how to allocate resources (time, people and money) that they hope will propel the company forward, towards its future. Many of these may be good, even great, decisions, but if the picture of the future isn't crystal clear, how can decisions really be evaluated? Standing in an imagined future can shift a leader's perspective, and consequently improve his/her decisions quite dramatically.

How does this work in practice? I remember chatting to the CEO of a global multinational mining group who had recently acquired an international asset. All efforts thus far had been going into aligning payrolls, salary scales and employee gradings with the South African based mothership. One conversation where we mentally travelled three years into the future, (which articulated the idea that the international asset rather than the South African-based asset would form the mothership of the group) revealed the folly, not to mention the enormous waste of time and resources that had gone into the alignment exercise. If anything, the South African assets should have been aligned to the new assets – exactly the opposite to what was contemplated prior to this simple but effective exercise.

A clear picture of the future is also an antidote to the complex mess of the current reality that most leaders deal with on a daily basis. One of our clients, busy with implementing a multitude of change initiatives including Continuous Operations (a change which impacts on the working times and arrangements of every single employee) was at a loss about how to deal with the resultant flagging morale, as well as explain how each initiative integrates and relates to the business's overarching purpose. This is an easy trap to fall into: leaders tend to be so obsessed with communicating a laundry list of "whats" that they omit the rest of the story: the context, the reason for the changes, and the imagined future.

Painting the future is as valuable for budding entrepreneurs as it is for big corporates. Many entrepreneurs are freedom fighters, overflowing with ideas, driven to innovate and create – on their own terms. Often, they also dream of building a business: a great dream, no dispute. But do they "go there" in sufficient detail to understand that with growth comes complexity, bureaucracy, management of people – a beast that needs to be fed – effectively removing the very freedom they originally fought so hard to attain? I've heard countless sad stories of people who have given up everything to get "there", only to eventually find out that the "there" is not what they wanted at all.

Where does painting the future intersect with traditional business school concepts like big hairy audacious goals (BHAG) and vision and mission? The perspective is different: vision and mission look forward, whereas painting a picture of the future enables you to look back FROM that future.

Vision and mission look forward, whereas painting a picture of the future enables you to look back FROM that future.

Vision and mission statements are often obscure, abstract, jargon heavy and forgettable. A picture of the future needs to be vivid. Emotional. Compelling. Inspiring. Something that imprints itself on your soul, makes you sit up, take note and yearn!

Lego blocks vs the Art of the Brick

Many years ago, I experienced Nathan Sawaya's mind-blowing *Art of the Brick* expo. Nathan uses the basic unit of a Lego block to create compelling artworks ranging from the Mona Lisa to the Golden Gate bridge.

I remember returning home and looking at Zack's Lego blocks reverentially, a tad mystified that these were the self-same building blocks that made up Nathan's brilliant creations – which were brilliant not because of the Lego blocks he used, but because of how he had put them together. However, while Nathan is no doubt a unique genius, Zack, by painstakingly following the process outlined in the Lego Manual, is able to build the Death Star, the Millennium Falcon, the London Bridge – and by so doing create something on a par with the *Art of the Brick*.

In many ways this analogy holds true for corporate strategy. Most companies may have the Lego blocks of their strategy, but have they put them together in a compelling, captivating, exciting way? Have they created a clear picture of the future they aspire to?

The good news is that companies do not have to be the Nathan Sawaya of corporate strategy – but like Zack, they do need to follow a process that will get them to their version of the *Art of the Brick*.

How?

There are those among us to whom painting a picture of the future comes as naturally as breathing. (In fact, CliftonStrengths® identifies a specific strength called Futuristic® which they describe as follows: "People exceptionally talented in the Futuristic® theme are inspired by the future and what could be. They energise others with their visions of the future. As if it were projected on the wall, you see in detail what the future might hold, and this detailed picture keeps pulling you forward, into tomorrow. Make the picture as vivid as possible. People will want to latch on to the hope you bring.")[50] If you are blessed enough to know someone who focuses most conversations on the future – treasure them. It's a perspective-shifting skill of unquantifiable value.

But what do you do if you see the value of painting a picture of the future, but simply have no idea how to go about it? (Call us for a THINKspiration Paint the Future Strategy workshop, or read the rest of this book – and you may not need to call us after all!)

Over the years, we have developed and perfected our Paint the Future process. It is based on a methodology called Structured Visual Thinking™, generously shared with us by UK consultancy Group Partners (who have worked with Disney, Pixar and Coca-Cola to name a few global giants).

I first encountered John Caswell and Hazel Tiffany from Group Partners in 2006, while I was still an executive at Harmony. At the time I was the lead on Project Zero, which involved redesigning the organisation from the ground up, working together with McKinsey.

About six months into the project I realised that our team's outstanding analysis and excellent insights, rather than lighting up conversations with my fellow executives, were sitting dormant in the hefty blue slide decks that McKinsey (and most other management consultants) are renowned for.

I instinctively knew that we needed to ignite this conversation about the company's future. But how? And with whom? Enter John and Hazel, who flew out from London and blew us away with their Structured Visual Thinking™ process.

It involved a comprehensive conversational architecture designed by Hazel. John, an artist, illustrator and design thinker then artfully facilitated the conversation while visually capturing it on the walls of the venue. As the executive team sat in an open circle I literally saw the conversation about the future come to life, as John "painted" it on the (white papered) walls.

John, Hazel and I bonded as likeminded souls do, and remain friends to this day. With their full support I adapted their methodology to suit my skills and deficiencies (primary of which was my absolute inability to write legibly, let alone draw). Over the years our THINKspiration team have adapted, shaped, and refined it to include and accommodate the power of visual and oral storytelling and foundational principles of Appreciative Inquiry, among other learnings.

I literally saw the conversation about the future come to life

So what does a typical Paint the Future Strategy workshop framed by the Structured Visual Thinking™ methodology entail?

Structured conversations

We facilitate a series of structured conversations that cover all the strategy bases with the top team. For instance we discuss the business's existing resources, assets and infrastructure; market forces and how the business can make the most of them; the competitive landscape, and what the competitors are up to; the business's stakeholders (including customers, shareholders, employees and others) – specifically their "pain points" and how the business can address these.

After that, we home in on what does or could make the business different and unique. Without fail, the most significant conversation with any team is about strategic outcomes (what we call the Big Win). This is about the team articulating what they want to achieve both financially and non-financially five years into the future. This is also where we talk about the "why" of the business – its purpose and how that connects to employees' WIIFM.

As well as the hard numbers and deliverables, the team discuss their aspirational culture and leadership blueprints in vivid detail. These, although highly aspirational, are always written in the present tense and in plain, everyday language. No jargon is allowed! We never use a $20 word where a $5 word will do. These words serve both as beacons of the future as well as daily reminders, which with repetition start to seep into the language of the business and are literally spoken into being.

Finally, after a mental "step back", the team ask themselves the key question that links all the conversations together: "If that is what our compelling future looks like, given where we are right now, what do we need to focus on to get us to where we dream of going?"

We overlay these conversations with the S.O.A.R (Strengths, Opportunities, Aspirations, Results) lens from Appreciative Inquiry, which ensures that the conversations are generative, and solution-focused, as opposed to being analytical and reductive.[51] This is important because our aim is to stimulate and engage imaginative, conceptual thinking rather than analytical reductive reasoning.

It's about imagination, not analysis.

The visual analogy

During these sessions we use a "mountain we want to climb" visual analogy. This stimulates participants' creative thinking and enables the leadership team to engage with the topics from a different perspective. Discussing the business's base camp versus competitors' base camps; potential external forces (like bad weather) that need to be dealt with; what "sponsors" and other stakeholders are expecting, ignites insightful conversations.

We work with the team to name their summit, their "big win" for the business within a five-year time horizon. From the perspective of their summit, the team flesh out their picture of the future: what does the summit look like and what will it feel like when they reach it? What does the rest of the world look like from the top? What overarching purpose propelled the team to conquer the mountain and reach the summit? As well as enhancing creative thinking, the analogy requires the team to develop their storyline and join the dots of their strategy in an integrated, logical and compelling way. The fact that in most cases none of the participants have ever climbed a mountain functions as a great equaliser among team members.

Thinking out loud together

The secret ingredient of all good conversations, but especially of constructive strategy conversations, is to create an environment where participants feel safe enough to "think out loud together about the company's future". These conversations among the leadership team are incredibly valuable. Team members can clearly articulate their thoughts and misalignments can be identified. The visual analogy stimulates dialogue, from which many, "Oh, I don't see it quite like that, but rather like this," clarification moments emerge.

"Paint the future" conversations require an optimistic bent. Critical, devil's advocate type deliberations do have their place – but not in these sessions! Although rooted in the current reality, we deliberately frame the discussion with a "what works" lens. Underpinned by the philosophy that we move in the direction that we ask questions about, we look for stories and examples of what works and try and figure out: how could we have more of that?

A "what's working" conversation enlivens, strengthens and energises. It's not about rose-tinted glasses. It's about identifying the green shoots of possibilities to build on. These types of conversations lead to new ideas, deepen connections, strengthen relationships and inspire.

> These types of conversations lead to new ideas, deepen connections, strengthen relationships and inspire.

They are in short, conversations about the future that are well worth having!

Chapter 5: Listen to where your people are

Listening forms the bedrock of an effective corporate strategy

In her well-known TED talk, Chimamanda Ngozi Adichie talks about the "danger of a single story"– making the point that to truly connect with people from different backgrounds one has to understand their world.[52] How does this apply to corporate strategy? Yes, strategy is the well-told story of a company's future – but it cannot be a single story. It needs to have multiple connection points so that employees are able to make it their own. Much like a Rubik's cube, leaders need to encourage employees to turn the strategy over in their minds until each employee's WIIFM slots into place.

So, rather than starting with the strategy message, leaders need to start by knowing their audience. This is the secret to influence and persuasion – without it, strategy communication becomes irrelevant clutter.

Many years ago, as undergraduate communication students, we were taught about the sender-receiver-feedback model which had been adapted from the engineering sciences. This model's fatal flaw is that it starts with the sender (rather than with the receiver), entrenching the single story, and effectively bypassing real, relevant issues that are top of mind for employees. The result: a disengaged, disgruntled group, so distracted by a mental "ticker tape" of their unheard issues that it's impossible for any new information to penetrate.

Knowing one's audience allows leaders to "walk a mile in their moccasins" (to quote Harper Lee in *To Kill a Mockingbird*).[53] The benefits of this approach to the organisation are profound: firstly, employees feel respected and validated when they are listened to and believe that their opinions matter. Secondly, for leaders, being able to understand the world from a different perspective changes how they think about their own. Thirdly, knowing where the audience is coming from allows leaders to acknowledge and speak into specific issues. The mere act of acknowledging issues (prior to even acting on them) melts them away – leaving the audience with the mental and emotional space to process and accept new information.

The mere act of acknowledging issues melts them away

Crafting a multi-dimensional strategy narrative that includes different viewpoints sounds tricky because leaders aren't used to doing it. Instead of giving in to the temptation to shy away from talking about the "bad" stuff, leaders need to face the fact that just because people aren't saying it, doesn't mean they aren't thinking it. Speaking into the issues, no matter how unpalatable they are, is an incredibly powerful leadership tool – one that is non-negotiable if a leader's aim is for their employees to personally connect with the corporate strategy.

Story listening

Listening to employees' stories catapults leaders into their world and helps them to understand their experiences in a much deeper and more insightful way. Stories help leaders to grasp and understand not just the facts but the emotion experienced.

It's often not just what is said, but what remains unsaid that results in an aha moment.

Because leaders may not have used or honed their story finding antennae, they may feel stumped by this issue. Yet stories are constantly unfolding in their midst – at work, at home and with friends. Being deliberate and intentional about excavating stories isn't that hard: my simple recipe is to either tell one of my own (which often triggers the "that's nothing" effect) or alternatively to ask "what happened?"

In the 20 years in which we at THINKspiration have used our story listening methodology (which we call Listening Sessions) to "go to where the people are" we never cease to be amazed as to how much the respondents enjoy these sessions and feel validated by being heard. Often reluctant at first, they almost always end up thanking us wholeheartedly after the session.

Listening Sessions reveal how employees think and talk about the business, which is vital input in terms of creating a relevant and resonant visual analogy that "feels like us". Perhaps even more importantly, Listening Sessions prod employees at all levels to actively think about the business – which I have come to realise is an essential first step towards engagement.

Story powered culture transformation – change the stories, change the culture

If we define culture as "the way we do things around here", what better way to understand it than via employees' stories? Stories offer authentic, real-time representations of what's actually happening. We often ask participants in THINKspiration Listening Sessions about their company's unwritten rules; in other words, "If I had just started working here today, and you had to get me up to speed in two minutes, what are the three things I need to know about how things work?"

Answers are telling, but further probing is often needed to get to the story level. So, if a participant says, "Play nice," I'll say, "Please give me an example?" A story or two or three is inevitable!

Our THINKspiration approach to culture transformation can be aptly summarised in the phrase, "Change the stories, change the culture." During Listening Sessions we encourage employees to share their stories which encapsulate the "from" culture (i.e., the existing or current culture that most organisations want to change) as well as the "to" culture (i.e., the aspirational culture – which does need to have some connection to what currently exists). Discovering and incorporating these stories within the business's greater strategic narrative plays a crucial part in making the strategy resonant, relatable and legitimate in the eyes of the employee audience.

The value of speaking into anti-stories

For every story there is an anti-story. Think about any change initiative you have been exposed to: no matter how well articulated, how convincing, there are always employees who will respond with: "I've seen this movie before. You said all this three years ago, and nothing happened. We haven't got the skills for this. Why don't you rather focus on X, Y, Z?"

This is a typical anti-story. An anti-story is a powerful, entrenched view that opposes what the business is trying to achieve. It is surprisingly difficult to counter an anti-story by using logic, facts and rational arguments, because these just trigger the "push back" confirmation bias impulse that most of us automatically default to.

The best way to deal with anti-stories is to speak into them directly.[54] As counter-intuitive as this sounds, by directly addressing the anti-story, leaders disempower the hold it has over employees' thoughts. Like ice in the face of heat, resistance literally melts away.

Most leaders, however prefer to stay on message and avoid contentious issues. While this may feel safer, sadly it inhibits real, authentic connection with their followers. Bravely "going there" – especially when "there" involves thorny, controversial subjects – is part of every leader's job.

When Steve Jobs launched iCloud in 2011, after briefly explaining the concept and the benefits, he confronted one anti-story directly in the following way: "So you might be thinking why should we believe them? After all, they're the ones that brought us Mobile-Me?" (By all accounts a complete disaster). The crowd reaction to this says it all – they laughed the way you laugh when someone has just articulated exactly what you are secretly thinking. Steve goes on to say: "It wasn't our finest hour, but we've learnt a lot." He then continues to extoll the virtues of iCloud. From that moment on, he has the audience in the palm of his hand, and he takes them exactly where he wants them to go.[55]

I clearly remember Bernard in his days as the CEO of Harmony marshalling the power of the anti-story: Harmony had just completed the hostile takeover of Randfontein Estates and were not winning any popularity contests among employees, especially middle management. Nonetheless, Bernard decided to hold a roadshow with this very group.

The atmosphere in the room was openly hostile, but Bernard was undeterred. He was armed with anti-stories thanks to the story listening work that we had done prior to his session. He was as blunt as I've ever seen him: "So you're probably thinking, here come these Harmony a**holes, Nazis in denim, ready to rape and escape – take what they want and leave you with nothing. And yes, I have to admit we haven't covered ourselves in glory with some of our recent acquisitions. But we have learned a lot – and I can tell you that the reason we fought so hard for Randfontein is that we believe in these assets, we believe in the ore body and we believe in you. We have got big dreams for Harmony – we want to change the industry and maybe even take over the world, but we can't do it without you."

The audience literally sat up, moved forward, made eye contact, and a session that had started out with reluctant rebels ended with a standing ovation from new converts.

The value of future culture aspirational stories

Any leader who intends to change the culture needs to gradually yet deliberately move the dial away from anti-stories and towards more positive, aspirational stories. Because humans are wired to see the negative, focusing on the positive needs to be a deliberate process.

At THINKspiration part of our story-powered culture change process involves us listening for and eliciting stories describing instances where the aspirational culture may already be happening. By creating a conducive environment, we encourage employees at all levels to think about examples of where they have seen the company's aspirational culture, for instance, "constructive dialogue" or "safety because-we-care" in action.

The idea is that these stories are collected with the aim of making them "go viral" throughout the business. As we know, stories are shared as much around the watercooler, the coffee station and the change house, as they are in more formal settings. The beauty of stories is that they create their own momentum: once they trigger the "that's nothing" effect, more positive stories follow. What starts out as hard work at the outset blossoms into a positive culture change process that feeds off itself – thanks to the stickiness and power of stories.

Chapter 6: Distil your strategy* into a compelling story and visualise it

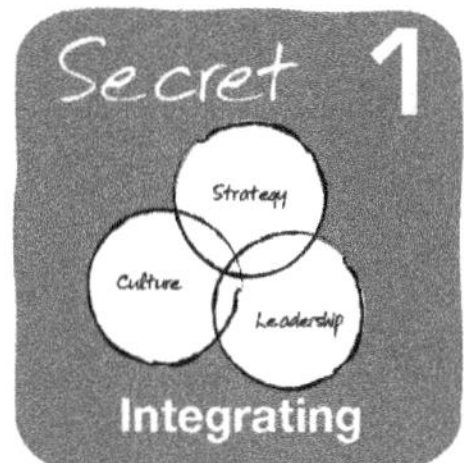

The power of why: tell the story of your choices and decisions

Just like stories, strategies need to make sense. Would you continue to watch a movie or series which was merely a collection of random action sequences, without an overarching plot? It's unlikely because the plot is the underlying logic, or the reason why the action takes place.

The plot provides meaning and context. It also sparks our emotions. It makes us care about what happens next. And yet most communication regarding strategy focuses primarily on the outcomes, on the "what" that has already been decided. The logic of the reasons for the choices (the "because of this we are doing that") is lacking.

Without the strategy "plot", even the most impressive list of action steps becomes confusing and meaningless clutter. In these complex times where companies are thrust into dealing with everything from digitisation to ESG to stakeholder activism, it's up to leaders to simplify, integrate and make sense. Leaders need to make meaning, rather than to overload already frazzled employees with yet another initiative.

** The future you want to create, in terms of strategy and culture, plus your insights into where your people are currently*

Without knowing the "why", the "what" is difficult – if not impossible – for employees to remember. For leaders it's a simple mistake to fix: sharing the strategic logic underlying a set of decisions isn't difficult. It doesn't take long. And it's an invaluable skill and habit for every leader to acquire.

Without the strategy "plot", even the most impressive list of action steps becomes confusing and meaningless clutter.

Our Australian partners, Anecdote, have a Strategy Clarity Story Framework which is a very useful tool in this regard – here's how it works:

Step one: Talk about "in the past" and refer to the context and recent history related to the decision/choice (WHY).

Step two: Refer to "what happened" – the catalytic event that precipitated the strategic choice/the change (WHY).

Step 3: Briefly describe the "so what we are going to do now", outlining the actual decision/s (WHAT).

Step 4: Outline the "imagine if", i.e., the dream – what we hope to achieve as a result of this choice (WHY).[56]

The aim here is to create a punchy "elevator pitch" narrative that communicates not only the "what" (i.e., the decision) but the plot around the "what" (i.e., the "why"). This enables leaders to make sense for their followers by joining the dots from the messy present to the imagined future in a concrete, coherent and simple way.

Below is an example that one of our mining clients used a few years ago when they implemented a new policy of mandatory reverse parking at head office (where it had previously only been mandatory on site at the mining operations).

In the past reverse parking was mandatory only on site at mining operations, which as we all know makes sense due to the potential safety hazards (i.e., fires/explosions) which would necessitate a quick getaway were they to happen. (Step 1)

Of course, it's highly unlikely that any of those hazards are applicable in a head office environment. However, "one team, one dream" is a way of working that we aspire to – and we want to do everything possible to make it a reality, to make head office and the operations feel like and function as one team. (Step 2)

Making reverse parking mandatory is a small but very visible and tangible way of reminding all of us at head office that our role is to be part of a bigger team located at our operations. (Step 3)

Imagine what kind of company we could create if we really lived "one team, one dream" on a daily basis. (Step 4)

The stickiness of stories

Cast your mind back to the last dinner party you attended, or even the last barbeque (during this new era of physical distancing and isolation, this may be an impressive feat of memory!) What happened? People gathered, conversation flowed and most likely you left with more than a few stories to tell. I'm betting that at no point did your host haul out his/her laptop and run you through a few slides to get the party started!

In most workplaces when employees gather around the coffee station or the water cooler – it's hard to get a word in: whether it's about the plight of the local rugby/cricket/soccer team, the hottest new series being streamed or the latest meme or joke. People are animated, engaged with their stories and each other, passionate about their opinion and about sharing it!

Fast forward to the PowerPoint presentation later in the day which outlines the way forward for the business over the next year. Unlike the movie or sport plot lines above, this directly affects the audience. Each and every employee has an active role to play in making or breaking it. Yet the discussion afterwards is lukewarm at best and often non-existent, and by the next day the presentation is all but forgotten.

The reality is that strategy is stuck on the flipchart, incarcerated in the corner office or imprisoned in the PowerPoint deck, while life inside most companies continues blithely in its absence.

Strategy is stuck on the flipchart, incarcerated in the corner office or imprisoned in the PowerPoint deck

It's little wonder that only 10% of all strategies are successfully implemented and that 75% of employees are NOT fully engaged.[57] [58] Employees have no idea of their company's "strategy story" and how what they are doing connects to the bigger picture. This conflation of factors directly affects performance – Gallup estimates that actively disengaged employees cost the US between $483 and $605 billion each year in lost productivity.[59]

Yet stories – more specifically business stories – can solve this problem! Let me remind you of the five reasons why:

- Stories are memorable and impactful
- Stories convey emotion and lead to action
- Stories create our identity, our culture and colour our destiny
- Stories convey authenticity, vulnerability and create connection
- Stories are influence tools that change people's minds

Compelling moments

The difference between a great story and a ho-hum story boils down to one word: compelling. So, what defines "compelling"? What makes something captivating? "Compelling" literally means, "I can't stop paying attention to it," while "captivating" indicates it has "captured my attention so completely that I am aware of nothing else." It's a challenging requirement, and difficult to pinpoint except by means of example.

Consider the following excerpts below:

From Martin Luther King's "I Have a Dream" speech:

I have a dream that one day on the red hills of Georgia the sons of former slaves and the sons of former slave owners will be able to sit together at the table of brotherhood.

I have a dream that one day even the state of Mississippi, a state sweltering with the heat of injustice, sweltering with the heat of oppression, will be transformed into an oasis of freedom and justice.

I have a dream that little children will one day live in a nation where they will not be judged by the colour of their skin but by the content of their character.

I have a dream today.[60]

"Compelling" doesn't have to be verbose, as demonstrated by John F Kennedy's pithy exhortation to, "Put a man on the moon by the end of the decade".[61]

And then there's one of my all-time favourites – from the Apple advertisement I mentioned previously, which features the following voiceover with images of global pioneers through the ages including Albert Einstein, Maria Callas, and the Wright Brothers:

Here's to the crazy ones. The misfits. The rebels. The troublemakers. The round pegs in the square holes. The ones who see things differently. They're not fond of rules. And they have no respect for the status quo. You can quote them, disagree with them, glorify or vilify them. About the only thing you can't do is ignore them. Because they change things. They push the human race forward. And while some may see them as the crazy ones, we see genius. Because the people who are crazy enough to think they can change the world, are the ones who do.[62]

Here's an example of "compelling" that is closer to home: I spent my early career in advertising, as a strategic planner. My job was to help turn a dry, complicated business strategy into a thirty-second piece of (radio or TV) art that would get the audience to jump off their couches and empty their wallets.

Ogilvy (an agency known for its creativity as well as its business nous) had a deceptively simple yet gruelling recipe that all strategic planners had to abide by. It was called "The Insight" and "The Argument".

"The Insight", as well as being a relevant, creative product insight, had to be a succinct and compelling one-liner that would inspire the creative team. "The Argument" comprised the rational substantiation for the claims made.

I remember working on one of my first campaigns for BabySoft toilet paper – whose unique proposition and single-minded message was "softness". As I bumbled my way through my thoughts about the insight during our strategy review meeting, I was cut short by the then creative director Alan Bunton (an industry veteran): "I think what you are trying to say is something like 'It's a Cadillac for your bum,'" he interjected – a brilliant, compelling insight that resulted in a simple, powerful and award-winning ad.

A compelling narrative triggers the "Netflix moment": a mini-movie starts playing in our mind's eye. We visualise. We empathise. We feel. These are concrete, emotional and memorable moments. Sadly, by allowing abstract jargon to run riot most corporate strategies miss the mini-movie boat. Can you picture a "create value for all stakeholders" mini-movie? Try as I might (and I have!) my mental screen just fades to black!

A picture speaks a thousand words

Early in 2010 we were contacted by a copper mine in the DRC (Ruashi, then part of Metorex) who were keen on a Visual Map intervention. Theirs was the big story of the DRC at the time and we were really excited at the prospect of working with them.

Of course, it inevitably meant visiting the mine, just outside Lubumbashi – which was not really on my bucket list, but Bernard reassured Adam (our resident THINKspiration artist) and me with, "Relax, it's like Welkom," a very civilised gold mining town in the Free State.

As excited as I was about the job, and the challenge of communicating corporate strategy and culture to a majority French speaking workforce, I'm a bit of a travel ninny. London, Paris and New York are my comfort zones – deep, dark Africa with its heart of darkness is not. Nonetheless I put aside my misgivings and forged ahead.

A few days before departure, only hours before we were due to get our vaccinations, I had a conversation that changed everything. Chatting to a friend who also happens to be a medical doctor, I mentioned in passing that I was off to the travel clinic. My friend, aware of an underlying medical condition I have, said: "WHAT? There's no way you can get those vaccinations. It's a total no-go!"

It was a convenient excuse for a travel ninny, but a disaster for our business. How could we do this job without me physically visiting the mine and meeting the people? SuperAdam to the rescue!

Not only did Adam travel to Ruashi without me – he saw the mine, met the people, and captured everything – and I mean everything – visually. When he returned, we spent hours poring over his beautiful detailed sketches of the people he had met and the places he had visited.

Each sketch was a masterpiece – capturing his unique perspective and insight. I only saw the sketches once, but they were so vivid and so memorable that I often have to stop myself and mentally check – I haven't ACTUALLY been there, have I? By the way, I can confirm, (thanks to the sketches) Lubumbashi is nothing at all like Welkom! Adam wholeheartedly agrees!

Pictures accelerate understanding. Imagine if I asked you to picture a well-known 20th century American. He has a high forehead, strong nose and dimple in the centre of his chin. There is a calm yet piercing quality about his eyes. Perhaps the most memorable feature is his hair, swept back from the face, thick and curly, cut just below the ears. Who this is? Turn the page to find out.

How did you do with this? If indeed you got the answer as a result of the written description, then perhaps it took you forty seconds (as it does most people). When you looked at the picture, you probably got it instantly. This exercise shows why pictures are so powerful: every word of the description is open to misinterpretation, but the picture conveys exact meaning much faster.[63]

Can you "pink elephant" your strategy?

If I had a dollar for every time anyone told me "I'm a visual person," I may well have been writing this on an island in the Caribbean! (I'm not!). All humans think visually. Tell me "Don't think of a pink elephant," and my mind overflows with pictures of pink elephants because the mental picture is far stronger than the word "don't".

Imagine if you could "pink elephant" your corporate strategy. The good news is – you can

Imagine if you could "pink elephant" your corporate strategy. The good news is – you can! By distilling your strategy into a compelling analogy or story and visualising that story, you are combining two methodologies (stories and visuals) that are scientifically proven as best practice in terms of memorability and retention.[64]

The pyramid of visualisation

As powerful as pictures may be, when it comes to effectively communicating strategy and leading for engagement, not all pictures are created equal. I've seen pictorial depictions of businesses, often computer generated, which – while they visually show some aspects of the business – are little more than abstract diagrams (which admittedly are still better than abstract words). However, these fall way short of the mark in terms of "distilling the corporate strategy into a compelling, inspiring story of the company's future".

Figure 5: Albert Einstein[66]

I find having our THINKspiration Visual Maps compared to infographics or visual capturing disproportionately irritating. But until I came across Zhang's pyramid of visualisation (which I have adapted slightly) I couldn't clearly articulate why. It classifies various visual representations according to some key aspects in which they differ from each other.[65]

Figure 6: The pyramid of visualisation.[67]

At the base of the pyramid we find the simplest of visual techniques, which are visual notes or visual capturing: an example of this would be live capturing during conference presentations, which graphically captures the main points and their relationship to each other on one page.

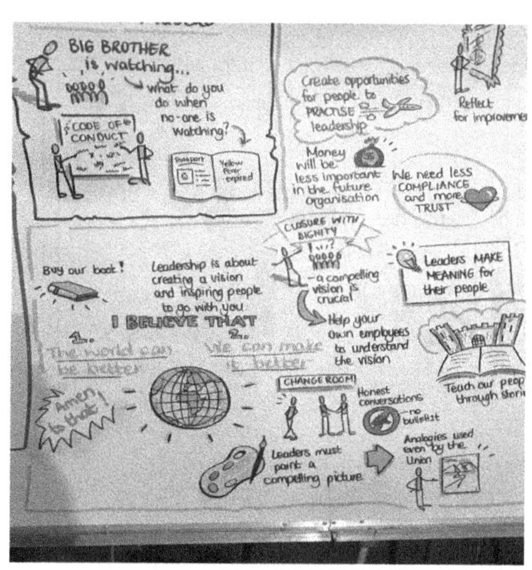

Figure 7: Visual capturing. Source: THINKspiration

The next level in the pyramid is icons: these are visual symbols that help us navigate through life without using words. They are graphic symbols and may be used to visually depict concepts where it is assumed that people know exactly what they mean (for example, road signs). Icons are often used to capture concepts like organisational values, but their effectiveness depends on shared understanding and meaning that is created around the icon.

Figure 8: Icons. Source: THINKspiration

The third level in the pyramid is visual images/storyboards: these are drawings or photos that convey a brief story. They go beyond visual notes or icons because they capture movement and motion.

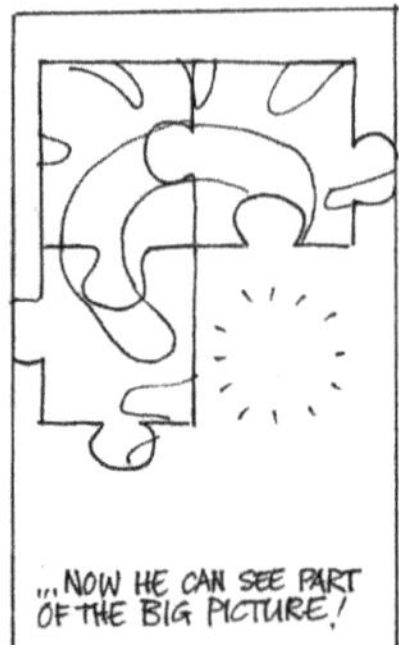

Figure 9: Storyboard. Source: THINKspiration

The fourth level in the pyramid is infographics: these are basic computer-generated graphics. They consist of facts that are presented as a picture which makes sense at a glance.

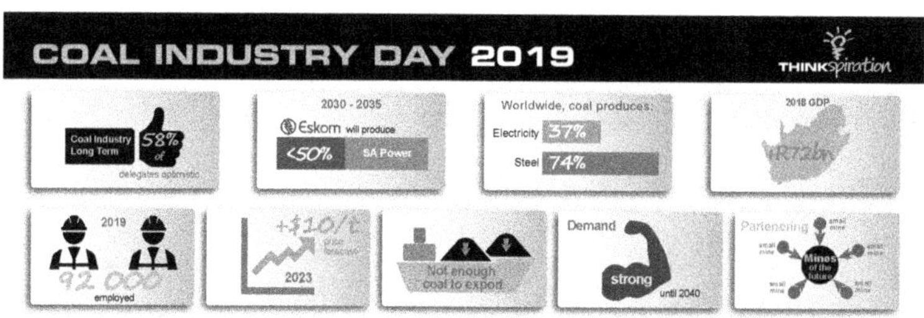

Figure 10: Infographic. Source: THINKspiration

The fifth level in the pyramid is conceptual illustrations: these are the visualisation of a system with multiple components, such as a graphic representation of a customer interface process showing multiple touchpoints. These illustrations create understanding of the whole system or the big picture and show how one part of the business integrates with or depends on another.

Figure 11: Conceptual Illustration[68]

The sixth level of the pyramid is a visual analogy or story: this facilitates the simplification of new or complex information by comparing it with something already known or understood. Metaphor or analogy based visuals do graphically what zip files do to computer data – they effectively shrink-wrap large amounts of information into manageable, understandable and usable formats.

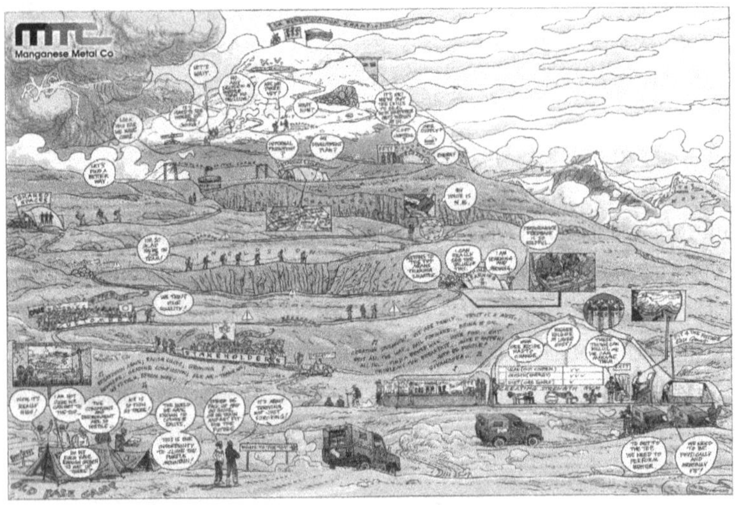

Figure 12: Visual analogy - MMC Visual Map. Source: THINKspiration

Visual analogies are a shortcut to understanding

In the early hours of August 8, 1963, an intrepid band of robbers hot-wired a six-volt battery to a railroad signal near a town about forty miles from London. The engineer spotting the red light ahead slowed his train to a halt and sent one of his crew down to investigate. Within minutes, the gang of robbers overpowered the train's crew and in less than twenty minutes made off with the equivalent of $60 million in cash.[69]

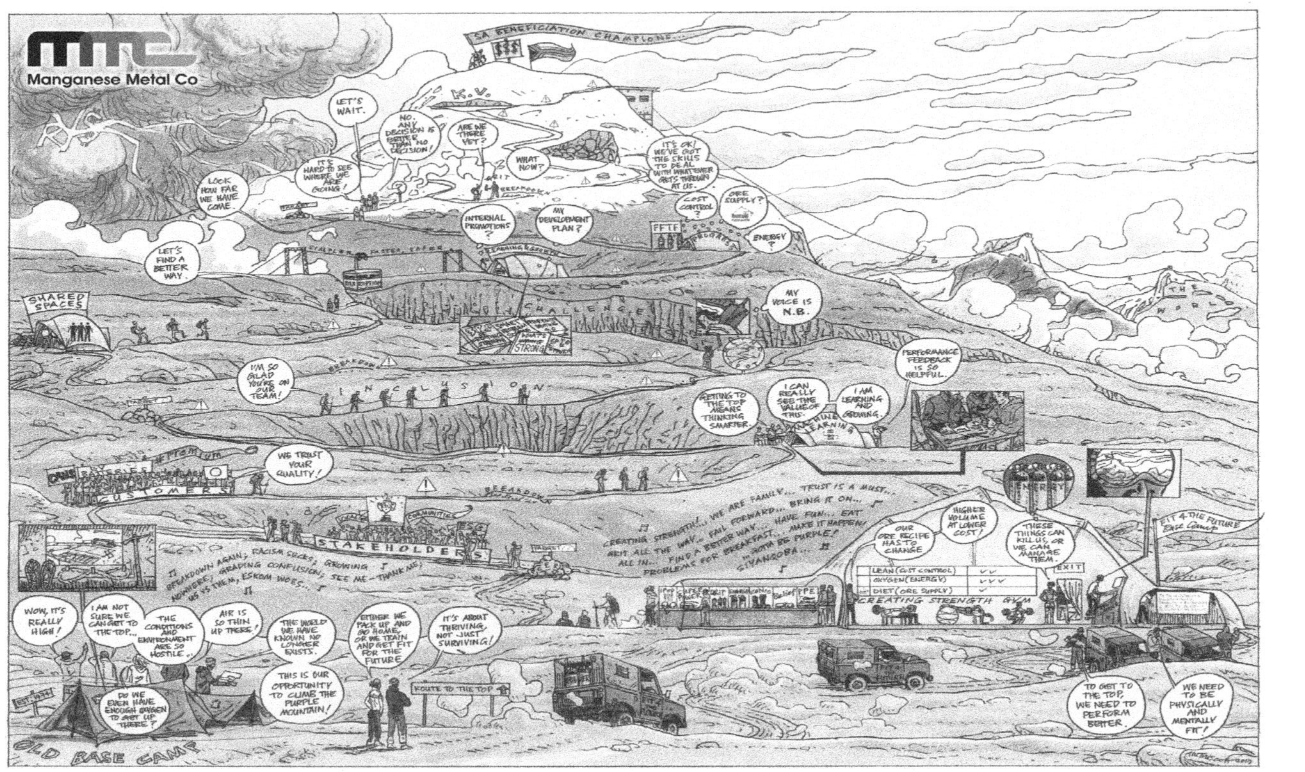
Manganese Metal Co
SA BENEFICIATION CHAMPIONS...
K.V.
LET'S WAIT.
NO. ANY DECISION IS BETTER THAN NO DECISION!
ARE WE THERE YET?
WHAT NOW?
IT'S HARD TO SEE WHERE WE ARE GOING!
LOOK HOW FAR WE HAVE COME.
IT'S OK! WE'VE GOT THE SKILLS TO DEAL WITH WHATEVER GETS THROWN AT US.
COST CONTROL?
ORE SUPPLY?
ENERGY?
INTERNAL PROMOTIONS?
MY DEVELOPMENT PLAN?
FFTF
LET'S FIND A BETTER WAY.
SHARED SPACES
CHALLENGE
STRONG
MY VOICE IS N.B.
PERFORMANCE FEEDBACK IS SO HELPFUL.
I'M SO GLAD YOU'RE ON OUR TEAM!
INCLUSION
GETTING TO THE TOP MEANS THINKING SMARTER.
I CAN REALLY SEE THE VALUE OF THIS.
I AM LEARNING AND GROWING.
LEARNING
WE TRUST YOUR QUALITY!
CUSTOMERS
STAKEHOLDERS
BREAKDOWN
CREATING STRENGTH!... WE ARE FAMILY... TRUST IS A MUST... GRIT ALL THE WAY... FAIL FORWARD... BRING IT ON... ALL IN... FIND A BETTER WAY... HAVE FUN... EAT PROBLEMS FOR BREAKFAST... MAKE IT HAPPEN! ... SIVANGOBA ...
BREAKDOWN AGAIN, RACISM SUCKS, GROWING NOWHERE, GRADING CONFUSION, SEE ME - THANK ME, US VS THEM, ESKOM WOES...
OUR ORE RECIPE HAS TO CHANGE
HIGHER VOLUME AT LOWER COST!
THESE THINGS CAN KILL US, OR WE CAN MANAGE THEM.
ENERGY
EXIT
FIT 4 THE FUTURE Base Camp
LEAN (COST CONTROL)
OXYGEN (ENERGY)
DIET (ORE SUPPLY)
CREATING STRENGTH GYM
PPE
WOW, IT'S REALLY HIGH!
I AM NOT SURE WE CAN GET TO THE TOP...
THE CONDITIONS AND ENVIRONMENT ARE SO HOSTILE...
AIR IS SO THIN UP THERE!
DO WE EVEN HAVE ENOUGH OXYGEN TO GET UP THERE?
THE WORLD WE HAVE KNOWN NO LONGER EXISTS.
THIS IS OUR OPPORTUNITY TO CLIMB THE PURPLE MOUNTAIN!
EITHER WE PACK UP AND GO HOME, OR WE TRAIN AND GET FIT FOR THE FUTURE.
IT'S ABOUT THRIVING, NOT JUST SURVIVING!
ROUTE TO THE TOP
TO GET TO THE TOP, WE NEED TO PERFORM BETTER.
WE NEED TO BE PHYSICALLY AND MENTALLY FIT!
OLD BASE CAMP

This famous heist became known as the Great Train Robbery and years later Bruce Reynolds, the mastermind behind it, referred to it as "my Sistine Chapel". For some, that comparison may seem as audacious as the robbery itself. Whether you agree with his viewpoint or not, his choice of analogy makes his point crystal clear.

As this example shows, an analogy is a comparison that shows a parallel (explicit or implicit) between two distinct things, based on the perception of a shared property.

Analogies permeate our daily lives and flavour our language: we fall in love, lose our grip on reality, observe one door opening as another closes, pass with flying colours, spill the beans, lose our marbles, sow our wild oats, knock their socks off.

Visual Maps – the secret to leading for engagement

A Visual Map combines the impact of pictures with the memorability of an analogy, creating a powerful multiplier effect. It forges the pathway to an unforgettable and indelible version of corporate strategy and culture among employees at all levels.

This is why Visual Maps are a tool at the heart of leading for engagement. They create the optimal environment for leaders to put the seven secrets into practice on a daily basis. Let's explore how they do this in more detail.

Visual Maps simplify, integrate and make sense of complexity (Secret 2)

Analogies and metaphors enable us to simplify complex information and make it memorable by comparing it with something we already know. Analogies function like zip files for data management, but are much prettier!

Analogies function like zip files for data management, but are much prettier!

An analogy or metaphor requires an in-depth understanding of the complexities of the business. By outlining the big picture, and connecting the dots, an analogy is the essence of simplicity on the other side of complexity. Because employees can see the "puzzle box lid" rather than just one or two disconnected puzzle pieces, they are empowered with the ability to make connections between concepts, constructs and systems. When employees are able to see the whole strategic picture – suddenly things start to make sense.

Why is simplification such a big deal? Because the clutter is real! To survive and deal with constant incoming information, our conscious mind simply switches off. But on an unconscious level our brains are still searching for meaning. In the same way that a powerful algorithm works to compress digital data and make meaning out of it, analogies function as a shorthand that simplifies, cuts through complexity and provides instant clarity.

Visual Maps tell a story – which is memorable, emotional and compelling (Secret 5)

Visual Maps capture the drama of the business. For a regionally based business that dreams of internationalising – the exciting Quest to reach New Galaxies. For a service and hospitality business that aims to differentiate itself through mind-blowing service delivery – the back-breaking behind-the-scenes work required to deliver The Greatest Show on Earth. These metaphors/analogies illustrate the struggles, threats, risks, opportunities and emotion of the business in ways that data never can. Analogies are compressed stories – and as such carry the elements that make stories so powerful – they are concrete, coherent, memorable, emotionally resonant and impactful. As we know, stories make your message stick! Visual Maps are unforgettable – once they are seen it's impossible to "unsee" them. At THINKspiration, we often catch ourselves in deep discussions with clients about complex elements of their business that have been captured in their Visual Map…and this is in the absence of the actual Map itself. Clients echo our experiences, saying the same – a Visual Map is like a movie that you can rescreen in your head, anytime you want to!

Visual Maps create a shared and inclusive language (Secret 3)

Using an analogy or metaphor in business works so well because it creates a shared language where none previously existed. This language, inspired by the analogy, is powerful because it gives employees a shared vernacular about what's happening, i.e., the mountain we need to

> Using an analogy or metaphor in business works so well because it creates a shared language where none previously existed

climb, the race we need to run, the tough terrain we need to conquer and our plan to achieve this - which is the essence of our strategy.

The shared language is also concrete – and the very antithesis of abstract MBA-like concepts (although it captures their meaning). This means that it is inclusive, regardless of education level, ability to speak English or position in the hierarchy. Leaders may initially view a Visual Map as a tool ideally suited for lower levels of the organisational hierarchy. While it does work well at those levels, we also get frequent feedback from our C-suite clients about how much better they understand their strategy thanks to their map!

Visual Maps catalyse curiosity and encourage storytelling (Secret 5)

All Visual Maps encourage storytelling. Sharing their own stories about concepts they see in the map enables employees to not only discover the story of the company, but also to connect their own story to it.

The map discussion is designed to stimulate curiosity and encourage problem-solving – essentially it's about orchestrating a series of aha moments among participants. They often make nonlinear connections – which expand their ability to think and reason. This is so important, because as we know, curiosity drives learning. So when employees discover insights themselves, they own them.

Everyone has a need to figure things out for themselves and come to their own conclusions, and so giving employees a chance to learn by discovery is critical to the internalisation of the map content.

Visual Maps spark stimulating and constructive discussions (Secret 3)

> Because analogies depersonalise issues, they enable constructive discussions that move issues forward

Because analogies depersonalise issues, they enable constructive discussions that move issues forward. I recall a large multinational conglomerate that we were working with several years ago. This client was waging an internal war on its own procurement department. Other departments could not access even the basic supplies that they needed, and all complaints to the procurement department seemed to go unheeded.

We created a Visual Map analogy that compared the business to a world-class soccer team who needed to prepare for their championship match within a series of locker rooms. One of these locker rooms, named Business Enablers, contained all the equipment the team would need for a soccer game – soccer kit, cones, balls etc. However, all of this equipment was depicted as behind a locked glass cabinet with a complicated lock and key system.

During the ensuing map discussion among procurement and other disciplines, the problem became clear to the procurement department. The analogy enabled them to see the issue from another viewpoint in a non-threatening way, resulting in a constructive and solution-oriented conversation.

Visual Maps align everyone to the big picture

(Secret 4)

One of the great lies of the executive suite is: "We have a strategy and we are all aligned to it." One of the reasons it's so difficult to align all levels of the organisation is because every level is at a different altitude. The executive level has a 30 000-foot view of the organisation. Middle management has a 10 000-foot view. As for employees at the coal face or the shopfloor – they are at ground zero and have no overarching or big picture view.

One of the great lies of the executive suite is: "We have a strategy and we are all aligned to it."

Add to this the complexity that results from each function understandably driving its own suite of initiatives: the HR executive who drives people development, the COO who drives operational excellence, the chief safety officer who drives safety. It's inevitable that no one individual really owns the whole – a key reason underlying fragmentation and complexity.

Having a shared picture of the future, and clear destination are the only way to solve for these issues. Shared meaning comes from a common picture that every person can relate to, and which enables every employee to see how and where they fit in. This creates an almost magnetic force-field for alignment between where the company is going and the contribution that each individual makes.

THINKspiration "Strategy to Story" Visual Maps

Every company has a story: its journey so far, where it is right now (and what it is struggling with) and where it wants to go – its hopes for an exciting future. Often this story is barely visible, buried in initiatives, overwhelmed by complexity, maybe even long forgotten. But it is always there – if you look hard enough. And the great news is that employees actually want to know about it, and be part of it. They want to go on a meaningful journey of discovery, progress and achievement.

Every company has a story if you look hard enough

Discovering and unearthing an organisation's strategy story (which may include its strategic ambition and commensurate initiatives, operating model, organisational effectiveness imperatives, safety and risk management strategy, values and culture transformation journey) and then applying an appropriate analogy to it is the core of what we do at THINKspiration.

We have created analogies:

- based on The Greatest Show on Earth where staff perform for their audience of clients,
- where teams are bravely taking on the challenge of scaling the heights of their Everest-like mountain,
- where they are road tripping (a la Route 66) – visiting different towns where they learn new skills to continue their transformation journey,
- where they decide to go "where no company has gone before" and embark on a journey through space towards distant yet exciting galaxies,
- where they endure an extensive training regime to get fit for their version of a World Cup Soccer Tournament.

There's no template, no one-size-fits-all. The analogy is chosen to match the client's strategy in fine detail. Every intervention must have its place. To do this effectively requires a thorough, insightful understanding of every facet of the organisation: its purpose, its plans, its ambitions, its dreams and, of course, its planned strategy to achieve these.

The Visual Map content architecture

As diverse as Visual Map analogies can be, they are underpinned by a consistent, coherent content architecture. This is based on what employees need to understand for their specific strategy and culture initiatives to make sense.

Employees, no matter their level, always need to know and understand the basics of how the business works:

- How do we keep score? How do we make money?
- How do we get our product to customers?
- What do customers value and why do they buy our product?
- What makes our product different to its competitors?
- Where are we headed? (strategic ambition/destination)
- Where have we come from, and why is that important? (journey so far)
- How do we describe our current culture? ("from" culture)
- How do we describe the culture we aspire to? ("to" culture)
- What do our strategic initiatives look like – and why are they so important? (these may be strategy, culture, operating model)
- What are our values?
- How do we define our leadership style?
- How does what I do fit in?

If you are wondering about whether the above process makes a difference to the bottom line, indeed it does. A large global engineering consulting business that we worked with have attributed their ability to successfully develop and implement a strategy to globalise the business and double its enterprise value to this methodology. In addition, they grew their share value by 130% and revenue by 70%. And not only did this process enable them to achieve organic growth, and expansion through M & A transactions – it also helped to transform the business from an inward-focused private company to a public company poised for an IPO.

The Visual Map prequel: the Feedback Visual

Star Wars do it. Disney does it. Even JK Rowling did it: maximise story power with a prequel. The corporate world is no different. The Visual Map prequel, which we at THINKspiration call the Feedback Visual, is a powerful picture with a specific purpose – to visually capture the current issues.

Star Wars do it. Disney does it. Even JK Rowling did it: maximise story power with a prequel!

Consider for a moment where the critical conversations about your business take place? Based on our experience, these happen in the hallway, the restroom, the watercooler, the change house, or the coffee station. It's in these informal settings that employees feel free to share what they really think.

Because we are external consultants who can't hang around businesses incognito, we use Listening Sessions to unearth these sentiments. Visualising these "current reality" issues of the day using a Feedback Visual works much like a cartoon does: it showcases the thorny issues in a wry, direct, yet palatable way. This candid mirror of reality never fails to resonate with employees – they take one look and admit (often amid relieved laughter), "Yes, that's us!"

Every business needs a tool which gives them the permission to have blunt, open, honest conversations – and air the anti-stories – and that's precisely what a Feedback Visual does. Feedback Visuals not only speak into the issues of the day (which some of our more salty clients call "putting the turds on the table") by inviting discussion – they truly make employees feel heard, seen and acknowledged. Feedback Visuals display the truth in a safe way and get every employee on the "same page" (literally), providing a common departure point for the journey towards an exciting future.

Chapter 7: Empower employees, from boardroom to shopfloor, to share the story

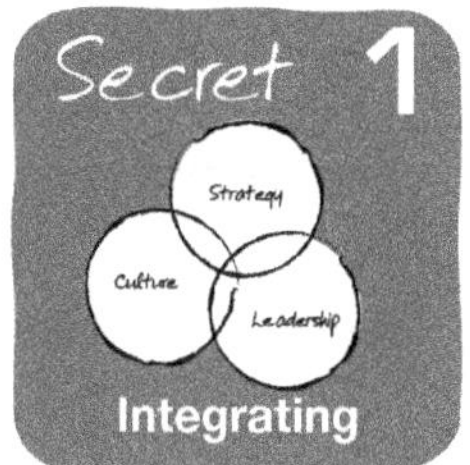

High quality conversations = high quality organisations

How would you rate the quality of conversation in your organisation? Do people talk constructively about the business, share ideas, come up with solutions? Or is it a moan fest about things that never seem to be resolved? Worse still, are employees actually interested enough, involved enough, engaged enough to talk about the business at all?

It makes sense that the quality of conversations that take place in an organisation and organisational performance are linked. So, for any business, a leading indicator of performance should be the quality of conversations employees conduct on a daily basis.

This resonates with my personal experience: during my time at Harmony my department conducted regular Listening Sessions with employees at all levels. We used to frequently amaze our more technically-minded colleagues by being able to accurately predict (due to the quality and content of these conversations) which shafts were heading for a performance crunch and which shafts were turning the corner.

The link between high quality conversations and business performance is not surprising: interactive discussion is one of the seven secrets of leading for engagement. The way a leader communicates is an integral building block of corporate culture. Yet, in many industries, leaders' communication styles seem to be trapped in an Industrial Age playbook.

Yet, in many industries, leaders' communication styles seem to be trapped in an Industrial Age playbook.

Think about the way meetings are run, the way questions are asked, the predominance of phrases like "all hands on deck", and acronyms like POLC (Plan, Organise, Lead, Control) and DAD (Decide, Announce, Do) that litter the mining and resources industries. One doesn't need a deep cultural immersion to discern the overpowering fragrance of command and control leadership that abounds. Financial services, telco and retail may have more evolved veneers, but are undeniably rooted in a similar vernacular.

Adding to this historical baggage, is the inescapable reality that most leaders have been promoted due to their ability to talk rather than listen, and most likely ascended the corporate ladder because they are "insanely technically qualified" (to coin a Tom Peters phrase) – rather than deeply skilled at engaging people. And yet, it's clear that leaders that are curious, listen deeply, ask insightful questions and who are authentic and vulnerable far outperform their more "Sergeant Major" style peers.

Leaders may well acknowledge this and even agree with it – but how can they practically change their ways? How do they switch from twenty years of barking orders at subordinates to asking "How can I help you?" Conducting a quality conversation, like asking an insightful question, may be a foreign skill for many leaders. Yet it's a skill that can be developed and honed. Once leaders understand the link between quality conversations and business performance they find it worthwhile to develop the skills required.

What prevents quality conversations?

In a word – okay, three – complexity, confusion and fear! Very few employees wake up, get out of bed and arrive at work to slack off, underperform or do a bad job. When people are enveloped in a cloud of complexity, overloaded with initiatives, bombarded with acronyms like ERP, BHAG or whatever else the flavour of the month happens to be – things don't make sense. And things which don't make sense erode trust and heighten anxiety, which is already pervasive because employees are afraid:

- That their contributions are not valid
- That their personal beliefs don't align with where the company is going
- That everything is changing and that they won't be able to adapt
- That they can't say what they really think
- That even if they see the value of doing things differently, there's no safe place to practice new ways of doing things.[70]

The command and control leadership style and the formality endemic to an S.O.S (Send Out Stuff) approach to communication reinforces fear rather than creating understanding and resolving anxiety. And so the vicious cycle continues.

How could leaders break this cycle and create an environment in which all employees understand how what they do creates value and contributes to the business?

Here's a practical exercise to try at "home": what percentage of time does your boss speak in meetings? When you meet with your team, what percentage of time do you speak? Generally the largest share of voice is directly correlated to position in the hierarchy.[71] The more senior you are, the more you get to speak.

The more senior you are, the more you get to speak.

So what happens when the boss leaves the room? Often the most insightful and valuable conversations follow. As mentioned earlier, Bernard, after forty years in the mining industry and twelve years as the CEO of Harmony, firmly believes that he learnt his most valuable lessons during his days as a young graduate in the miners' change house (changing room), rather than in the boardrooms of London or New York.

The change house was a place where the frontline workers would gather each day and engage in passionate discussions and debates about the company – what it was doing, where it was going, and what they could do to fix it. No bosses present meant that all voices could be heard.

Dialogue is the oxygen of change. Why?

Why is dialogue so critical to successful change? Because fundamentally curiosity drives all learning. So rather than leaders being fact-flogging talking heads, they need to focus on orchestrating a series of aha moments – asking the right questions, rather than having the right answers. It's quite a radical mindset shift for most leaders.

Leading for engagement requires leaders to get employees to think about the business, not to tell them what to think about the business. By presenting employees with key questions that they and the business are grappling with, leaders can demonstrate authenticity, vulnerability and strongly signal that they believe in the intelligence of employees and value their ideas and input.

This type of conversation may not yield the right answers at the outset. But by stimulating an environment where everyone feels safe enough to share their ideas and "think out loud" about the business, the quality of ideas and solutions – not to mention openness to change, buy-in and engagement – increases exponentially.

Dialogue drives internalisation

When we are asked to think deeply about something, we start to own our ideas and solutions – this is where and how the internalisation process starts. Employees need to think first, then internalise messages in order to act. Ownership powers thinking, and thinking powers ownership!

In addition to stimulating thinking, which invites ownership, discussion is so valuable because it is the most effective way for people to process and retain information. "Tell me, I'll forget, show me, I'll remember, involve me, I'll understand," is a well-known adage that we see demonstrated every time we observe a Visual Map discussion.

Asking questions vs. asking the RIGHT questions

While questions are a great tool to stimulate discussion – there are questions and there are good questions.[72] I'm sure most of us have been on the receiving end of rapid fire, interrogation-like questions: "did you do it? Did it work? Was it safe?" These are binary questions: there's an expected yes or no answer. Closely related to binary questions are stacking questions, which take you down a path of logical thought: "did you go? How long did it take? Who was there?" As you can see, these questions are not great conversation starters.

Leading questions, where you "lead" the respondent to the right answer are also not ideal, because people are smart and they will quickly know they are being manipulated.

What is a good question?

There are certain phrases that help. For instance, rather than asking: "Is it safe?" a leader could ask, "On a scale of one to five, how safe is it?" And then, "Tell me more," or "Say more," is encouraging and opens up the conversation. "What's in the way? Give me an example? Tell me about a time when… What am I missing?" are questions that will yield further insight.

All of these are good questions. But the key to insightful questioning is a mindset of deep curiosity about how the other person sees the situation and views the world. Leaders who are able to truly "blank" their brains, step inside others' shoes and see the world from an alternative point of view will see magic unfold.

But the key to insightful questioning is a mindset of deep curiosity about how the other person sees the situation.

Putting it into practice: The Map Discussion Manual (that also develops leaders!)

Where is my leading leading to?

Many companies may spend time and money on leadership training, but does the training capacitate leaders to align their employees towards the corporate strategy and culture? Does it equip leaders to ask the right questions? To stimulate the appropriate discussions? To move, engage and inspire employees?

Despite falling in love with every single Visual Map that I've worked on, I know deep down that it's not about the map! The real, sustainable value lies in the conversations that every map sparks: conversations at every level of the business between leaders and their teams, about the strategy and their contribution to it.

Leaders from the C-Suite to the shopfloor learn how to be skilled listeners, storytellers and facilitators of corporate strategy discussions.

Even more impressive is the way in which this tool catalyses real-time leadership development: leaders from the C-Suite to the shopfloor learn how to be skilled listeners, storytellers and facilitators of corporate strategy discussions.

For a leader, conducting a Visual Map discussion provides the perfect opportunity for development and growth. For a company, it's in this discussion that strategy, culture and leadership come together as a powerful and integrated whole bringing Secret 1 (integrating strategy, culture and leadership) to life.

The Visual Map "Strategy to Story" Discussion Manual

This is where the Visual Map starts to function as a leadership development tool. The Discussion Manual is carefully created according to best practice principles required to facilitate generative, constructive discussions and create environments of psychological safety.

Clients are often curious about where the magic lies, and I firmly believe that it's in the combination of positively framed and story-eliciting questions that form the foundation of the manual. We also inject a sense of fun and play into the questions, where appropriate and relevant to the Visual Map – and we have seen how participants appreciate and engage with these. This design assists the leader in allowing the conversation to flow.

Every manual is written to literally guide the conversation so that every element of the map is covered and discovered – not by the leader as "talking head", but by the leader as facilitator. Questions like "What do you think?", "Can you tell me about a time when… ?", "How might we… ?" ensure that the discussion is interactive, relevant, meaningful and richly flavoured with anecdotes and stories (which enhance memorability).

The manual functions like a script, and is designed to keep the discussion on message, ensuring that leaders feel secure enough to ask good questions rather than obligated to provide all the answers.

Getting the whole company talking about the right stuff

Line-driven roll-out

Role modelling is one of the most powerful leadership mechanisms. In most businesses, employees do as the boss does. To capitalise on this natural force, the Visual Map roll-out is cascaded via the line structure. The CEO and their immediate team kick off the process. They receive practical training and coaching to equip them to hold their own sessions with their direct reports. Those direct reports are then trained and coached to hold their sessions and so on – until every single employee is reached.

Every leader puts the principles of storytelling, listening and facilitating discussions into practice.

During the map conversations, every leader gets the opportunity to put the principles of storytelling, listening and facilitating discussions into practice. To keep leaders accountable and provide a tangible guideline we stipulate the 40/60 rule: this means that the leader/facilitator should not talk more than 40% of the time. Gradually, leaders start to realise that rather than telling employees what to think, the main aim is to get employees to share their thoughts, innovate, create and problem-solve.

Practising before performing – Visual Map training workshops

In my tennis playing days, my practice-to-match-playing ratio was about 90:10. I suspect that's true for most professional sports people. And yet when it comes to leaders practising before performing, I suspect that a 0:100 ratio might be more accurate. It seems to be a generally accepted norm that leaders rarely rehearse before presentations. And yet, what underlies the great, natural looking iconic presentations by a Barack Obama, a Steve Jobs, a Brené Brown? In each case, it's the same thing: practice! Not once or twice but hundreds of times.

If practice is a requirement for normal, run-of-the-mill presentations, it's even more important for a Visual Map discussion, which turns "this is the way we have always done it" on its head. Hence we run Visual Map Training workshops prior to the map launch and rollout.

A Visual Map Training Workshop creates a safe environment for leaders to practise "different" skills.

A Visual Map Training Workshop creates a safe environment for leaders to practise what may at first feel like "different" skills. After all, most leaders have not often facilitated discussions using a Visual Map, which tells the story of the business and what it dreams of achieving. What never ceases to amaze me is how leaders who may at first seem reluctant, after a few run-throughs, take to this like ducks to water. Because doing things differently is a risk, the training workshops are designed to minimise the risk that leaders feel and build their own confidence and trust in the process.

The Visual Map launch

Over the years, we have experimented with various launch formats, and without question the optimal design is to get all senior leaders together during the course of a normal working day for a brief plenary session, after which they break up into their functional teams. Venue-wise, a large hall with separate sections for functional team discussions works well. This approach is effective for a number of reasons:

- If I see everyone else doing this new thing at the same time that I'm doing it, it feels less scary.
- I can't just avoid discussing the Map and leave it languishing in my office. (Social psychologists would call these safety in-numbers and social proofing phenomena).
- It allows suspense and excitement to build.
- An on-site or near-site venue signals that this is something that is integral to the business – owned by "us" rather than yet another fancy off-site workshop with external consultants.

Ongoing conversations

The launch is only the beginning. Because Visual Maps contain references to every aspect of the business, they are the ideal tool to frame ongoing conversations about the business. These range from executive level corporate strategy conversations to daily team meetings among the frontline.

"If it's not on our map, why are we discussing it?"

There should be nothing that happens in the business that does not have a reference point on the map: as one of our clients puts it, "If it's not on our map, why are we discussing it?"

The map also becomes a powerful integrator for all employee communications: the visual icons in the map can be cut out and tagged onto all relevant internal communications going forward. This works extremely well because once they have been engaged through conversation with the map, employees remember the big picture. Then when they see a relevant visual icon they are able to automatically recall it and slot it into the context – with the result that the corporate strategy and its complex web of initiatives and plans, is simplified and finally starts to make sense!

IN A NUTSHELL

Indra Nooyi was the CEO of PepsiCo, a role she held for a dozen years until she retired in 2018. She attributes one of her greatest breakthroughs to "the ability to take something down to its essence and explain it in a way that's so simple and clear that whoever's listening can form a picture in their head."[73]

It's an incisive and succinct summary of great leadership, underpinned by a deep-seated belief system.

As a leader do you believe that:

- Once employees understand the big picture they are able to get excited about the journey, and keen to go on it?

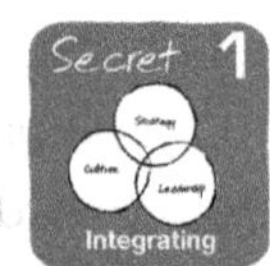

- If you can't explain it simply, you don't understand it well enough?

- Leaders are translators and sense makers? Employees will act on their own insights and not what leaders tell them? Success is not about a few people having better answers – it's about everyone engaging with the right questions?

- If you want your people to think about the strategy, you have to give them the whole story – the context. Once they understand it and see how they fit into it – they will align, and take responsibility?

- Strategy is an adventure, a quest. It needs to be stirring, have good guys, bad guys, struggles, setbacks, barriers. It needs to be an adventure that everyone wants to be part of?

- Striving to be the best version of yourself is far more effective than to trying to emulate anyone else?

- You need to listen to, understand and acknowledge the journey so far because people won't change unless you speak into their issues?

Believing is one thing, practising is quite another. For all of us. But if you can tick the box on most of the above, there's no doubt that you are a leader who leads for engagement and are well on your way to becoming the leader you are meant to be!

SEE IT IN ACTION: 1

A number of years ago, we got a call from one of South Africa's largest industrial companies, their frustration clearly evident. Having just been through a significant restructuring exercise, they had called in various big consultancy firms for this process. They had created a new operating model, a new vision, and an ideal/aspirational culture.

Being a firm of highly structured industrial engineers, they had spent the previous year trying various approaches to onboard employees, and to roll this out – including workshops and brown paper sessions. They were astute enough to realise that they were getting nowhere fast, and they were keen to try a different approach.

When we looked at their operating model it was evident as to why it wasn't catching on. Although a beautiful piece of theory, its abstract nature made it unattainable, forgettable and confusing – despite the highly skilled nature of the employees. The model consisted of two circles (specifying the objective of safe production, surrounded by the aspirational values-driven culture of accountability and high performance.) Embedded within these two circles was a four-quadrant matrix indicating the four key elements of the operating model: direction, governance and sustainability, business enablers, and people enablers.

We convinced this client to create a Visual Map, using a soccer analogy solidly underpinned by the facets of the strategy and culture.

Figure 13: Visual map using soccer analogy. Source: THINKspiration

As you can see (in the map above), this started with many of the different divisions of the business gathering in a parking lot and boarding a "One team" bus (communicating the strategic objective of unity). We see the bus on its journey to the World Industry Stadium, indicating the desired strategic objective.

Along the way, we see that the route holds challenges in the form of "safety" and "cost" potholes. We are privy to the mood and mindset of the passengers on the bus. This is where we enhance resonance by showcasing some of the current (negative) issues experienced by the employees. We see these in the form of the bus playlist, featuring songs such as "The Blame Game", and "Red Tape Rules".

10,000 SIGNATURES • RED TAPE RULES… IN THE ATMOSFEAR… I CAN'T DECIDE
DON'T THINK JUST TICK • TOO AFRAID TO FAIL
I'M TELLING YOU • THE BLAME GAME
WHO DUNNIT? • JUST SAY NO…
Congrats YYY: Industry Leaders in cost, quality and safe production…
FULL TIME
YYY TEAM
EXTERNAL THREATS
2
0
QCDSM
WORLD INDUSTRY STADIUM
BLENDING
LESS ASH
REDUCED FINE COAL
ROBOTS
BRIDGES
HOUSING
DIV
ROI
INZALO
$
GO TEAM
BONUS
SAFE
THANKS
Zero Harm!!
CUSTOMERS • COMMUNITY • SHAREHOLDERS • EMPLOYEES
WORLD INDUSTRY STADIUM
ZERO HARM
YOU CAN DO IT!!
PLAY THE BALL, NOT THE MAN!!
WELL DONE…
HOW CAN WE HELP?!!
SERVICES
SAFE COAL FACE
ethics always
WHAT DO YOU WANT TO ACHIEVE?
Direction
WHAT ARE THE RULES?
Governance /Sustainability
WHAT DO YOU NEED?
Business Enablers
WHAT MAKES A GOOD TEAM?
People Enablers
1 TEAM
HOW TO WIN
QCDSM
WAY OF THINKING
THIS IS THE MATCH OF OUR LIVES. LET'S PREPARE WELL BEFORE WE GET ONTO THE FIELD!!
WORLD INDUSTRY STADIUM
EMPOWERED
• NO FEAR
• DO MY BEST
• IF YOU FALL DOWN – JUST GET BACK UP
• THINK-DECIDE-DO
• NO ONE TO ASK
• ON MY OWN
• CAN DO!
• DON'T TAKE THE MONKEY
• I MAKE IT HAPPEN
• TIME TO LISTEN
• ASK DON'T TELL
• IT'S ALL UP TO ME (and I love it!)
• CONSIDER IT DONE
ACCOUNTABILITY

Eventually we see the bus arrive at the World Industry Stadium, and as the players disembark, they are confronted by a hand-drawn version of the operating model, explained to them by the coach. He makes sense of it by referring to it as their "How to win" game-plan. The players are then ready to enter the locker rooms in preparation for the big match.

Each locker room is specifically designed to represent one of the four quadrants of the operating model. The abstractions of "direction", "governance and sustainability", "business enablers", and "people enablers" are made concrete by means of specific situations such as, "Who gets a red card?" (governance and sustainability), and "Do we have the right equipment for the match?" (business enablers), thus giving employees at every level something to relate to.

Furthermore, the Visual Map shows the desired culture shift by means of an iPod "playlist" that the players listen to before going onto the field. We see the players play the game, and a scoreboard depicting competitors (in this case external threats). Company values are written on the field; and in the stands we see different stakeholders of the business watching the game and using banners to demonstrate their needs. The vision of the business is depicted as a banner flying overhead.

By expressing the strategy as a relatable and concrete analogy in picture format, all employees could see the big picture, with the result that all strategic, cultural and operational initiatives made sense. A crucial element of buy-in was the anti-stories (gathered via employee Listening Sessions) which are depicted on the map. By including these, the map was transformed from boardroom jargon to a co-created, co-owned and resonant vision of the future – that all employees understood, bought into and aspired to be part of.

The real magic of the process, though, was in the leader-led team conversations that every leader facilitated with their team. Not only did these make the vision and purpose come alive for every employee – the memorability and retention were so high that seven years later, during a chance encounter with a senior manager, he regaled me with the detailed content of the map, as well as his team's responses and reactions to it.

The map triggered heated yet constructive discussions – where solutions were debated and agreed upon. And it was rolled out from the top to entrench the importance of leadership role-modelling.

For this business, as for many others, using a Visual Map was a different way of discussing strategy – and whether at the C-suite or the coalface, the feedback was the same: "Finally, all this stuff (the strategy, culture, operating model) makes sense to me!"

Once rolled out team by team, the Visual Map became a powerful catalyst for ongoing conversations about the business, and leaders have used it to frame every meeting, from the executive to the frontline. This is living proof that it is possible to liberate strategy from the one hundred-slide PowerPoint deck and ensure that it is discussed on a daily basis at all levels.

This client used their Visual Map as a catalyst for gathering oral stories about their strategy and culture. These stories, gathered and re-told at every level of the organisation, helped to entrench a compelling picture of the desired future.

Results

While it would be wonderful to talk about the way this company's share price rocketed (it did), or about the safety and productivity improvements that it experienced, we all know that these achievements are the result of a number of variables coming together and can't only be correlated to the Visual Map process in and of itself.

However, the client was unreserved in his praise for the process: "This is the best tool I have ever used to make strategy and culture come alive – our Visual Map enables us to discuss any business concept at every level with ease and understanding."

SEE IT IN ACTION: 2

During January 2018, I met the new CEO of the Chevrah Kadisha for coffee. He had contacted me after reading my first book (*The Leadership Riptide and How to Escape*) over the Christmas break, and was excited to discuss some of the ideas I had outlined and how these could apply to his organisation.

The Chevrah Kadisha (the Chev) an NGO, is the largest social welfare organisation in the Southern Hemisphere. Beneficiaries of its many services include the elderly, the mentally disabled, the mentally ill, the physically disabled and orphans.

Functioning as the nucleus of the Jewish community, and solidly underpinned by its ethos, "No Jew gets left behind", meant that it had historically been well funded by donors in the Jewish community. However, over time it had become set in its ways, dominated by functional silos, mini-empires and resistance to change.

To complicate matters, the social and economic chasm between the mainly black staff and their far more affluent, white constituency of patients, residents and beneficiaries meant that staff engagement was at an all-time low, with divisive issues like racism and discrimination a common feature.

The new (and much younger) CEO was determined to do things differently. As we chatted and got to know each other during that first of many cups of coffee, I saw his passion and determination shine through.

His first move was to restructure the organisation – in the process removing unnecessary levels and promoting competent, capable people into leadership positions. With a new team at the helm, the stage was set for a customised THINKspiration intervention.

The board and donors required a clear and coherent strategy document, and the leadership team needed a methodology for effectively engaging employees in a series of conversations about an exciting future that they would want to be part of.

Paint the Future Strategy Workshop

Our first step was to conduct a Paint the Future Workshop to help the new team discover the Chev's purpose, and articulate its strategy and aspirational culture. The CEO, eager to create an opportunity for the new leadership team to bond, organised a two-day off-site strategy session.

Too often the most noteworthy aspect of these types of breakaways is the exotic venue rather than the inspirational insights. We wanted far more from the enthusiastic leadership team – and so carefully designed the two-day workshop, incorporating facilitated conversations around strategy, purpose and actionable outcomes.

An essential component of the discussions focused on culture. By doing projective, creative exercises, key words and concepts surfaced that formed the basis of the aspirational culture – which resulted in the Culture Print.

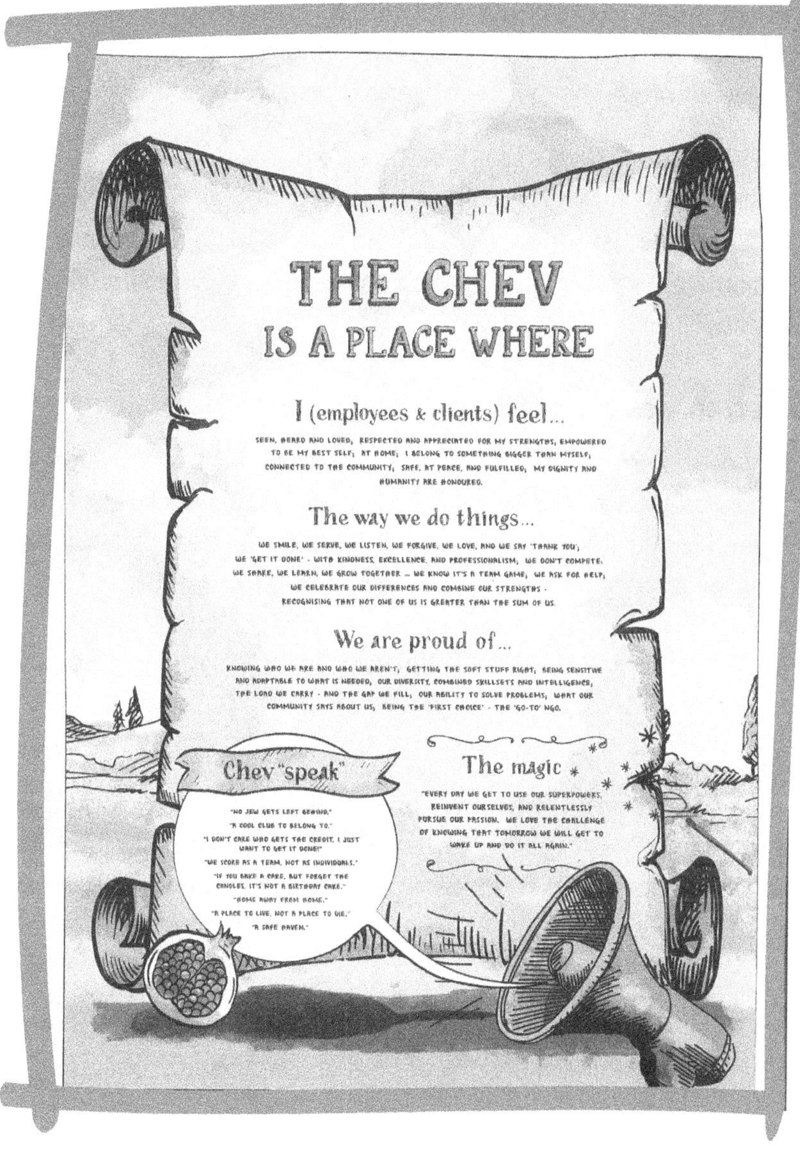

Figure 14: Chevrah Kadisha Culture Print. Source: Chevrah Kadisha/ THINKspiration

We discussed purpose and articulated the Chev's purpose statement as: "To provide a safety net for the Jewish community who find themselves in need physically and emotionally, so that they can improve their wellbeing and quality of life."

The third outcome was about the team discussing, debating and ultimately agreeing on what to prioritise and how to allocate resources (time and money) to make the future – as envisaged by the team – a reality. Eight strategic focus areas were identified by the team.

Listen to where the people are

This was the second part of our intervention and it was designed to listen to and convey the voices of employees at all levels. We conducted one-on-one Listening Sessions with identified opinion leaders at every level and from every segment of the Chev. Our team conducted these free-flowing conversations to understand the business from the eyes of that specific employee, to discover their views regarding "what's going well/strengths" and also to get them thinking in a positive way about the future.

In the twenty years in which we have used this methodology, we never cease to be amazed as to how much the respondents enjoy the Listening Sessions and feel validated by being heard.

Although these interviews took the form of individual conversations, common themes emerged. In the Chev's case there was a clear segmentation of specific issues relevant to the higher income earners and lower income earners respectively.

Based on the content, we created the Chev Feedback Visual: a visual summary of the feedback that highlights the current issues. While often predominantly negative in its content, this is a powerful tool in terms of speaking into the issues of the audience. When shared by leaders with employees in an honest and vulnerable way, it gets everyone on the same page – and clears the path to discussing the exciting future.

Discussing this feedback openly with employees is an act so rare, bold and courageous, that when the CEO shared the feedback visual with the Chev employees, one could hear the audience gasp and then exhale. The blessed relief of being listened to and heard at last!

Figure 15: Chevrah Kadisha Feedback Visual. Source: Chevrah Kadisha/ THINKspiration

Let's take a closer look at the Chev's feedback bus (the reason for a bus will be apparent once we see it in the context of the Chev's Visual Map).

Some highlights from the Feedback Visual include the solid chassis of financial stability and the loyal donors – which are seen as the wheels that propel the organisation forward. Compassion is widely regarded as the fuel of the business – and depicted as the petrol tank.

Some of the burning issues among employees can be seen in the soundtrack/playlist of songs. The clear division between how senior employees and lower level employees have different experiences is seen by the plusher top level of the bus and the lower level scruffier version. However even at the top, issues like silos and firefighting are prominent.

Lower levels have to contend with racism, questions regarding purpose (why am I here?) and being found to be guilty until proven innocent.

We see that the idea of "family" pervades the atmosphere, and there are positive signs of autonomy. Burnout is an unfortunate reality. In general, the issues are captured by the soundtrack, which depicts the mood and mindset on the bus.

The bus is moving forward, but it's not an easy road. The bus is slipping and sliding on the soft sand of fundraising challenges, negative publicity, dysfunctional state systems, and inadequate communication. But the signposts indicating Thuma Mina ("send me" in isiZulu) and Good Stories encourage employees to press on, and to do their best to change their world for the better.

Sharing this Feedback Visual with employees as a prequel to the Visual Map (ideally in the same session) enabled the leadership to acknowledge issues, and to create a feeling that "we are all on the same page". It afforded leadership an opportunity to openly and honestly acknowledge the issues. Most importantly, it set the scene for a constructive Visual Map conversation about an exciting future.

The Chev's Visual Map

Figure 16: Chevrah Kadisha Visual Map. Source: Chevrah Kadisha/ THINKspiration

The Chev Visual Map takes the form of the Chev Community Theatre – where the dedicated cast of characters (the employees) work together to contribute to the greater purpose of the Chev to serve its community. To showcase the strategy, the focus is on how a talented cast delight audience members with their production, "Home is where the heart is".

In the top right hand corner, we see the Chev employees embarking on their long journey to their workplace – "The Chev

CHEV COMMUNITY THEATRE
EST: 1888
IT'S HARD WORK BUT LOOK AT THE SMILES ON THEIR FACES!
PURE DELICIOUSNESS!
Nosh Café
THE FACILITIES ARE EXCELLENT!
IT TAKES ME SO LONG TO GET TO WORK – I'M ALREADY 5 MINUTES LATE & I CAN'T AFFORD TO LOSE MY JOB!
I KEEP THINKING OF MY ABBA & THIS INSPIRES ME!!
SAFETY NET FOR THE JEWISH COMMUNITY
HOME IS WHERE THE HEART IS!
I FINALLY GET WHY WE ARE HERE – TO MAKE OUR AUDIENCE FEEL HAPPY & SAFE!
WELCOME! EVERYBODY HAS A ROLE TO PLAY!
WHAT'S YOUR SUPERPOWER?
I LOVE THIS SHOW – IT'S BRILLIANT EVERY TIME!
ACT II FOCUS ON QUALITY AND CONSISTENCY
CHECK LIST Spots, smoke, mics, music
CHEV COMMUNITY THEATRE HOME IS WHERE THE HEART IS
WHAT'S THIS SHOW ABOUT?
WHAT'S MY ROLE?
TRANSPORT
IS THERE A PLACE FOR ME?
ACT III EFFECTIVE AND TRANSPARENT COMMUNICATION
THEY REALLY GET MY STORY!!
I FEEL SEEN HEARD AND LOVED!
I AM PROUD TO BE PART OF THIS FAMILY. I CAN'T BELIEVE I GET TO COME AND DO THIS AGAIN!
CAST • Caregivers • HR • Revenue • Social workers • Nursing • Kitchen staff
ACT I DEFINING SERVICE & PRODUCTS

SEE IT IN ACTION: 2

Community Theatre". Thought bubbles capture some of the thoughts of these travellers (depicting issues that emerged from the Listening Sessions).

We also see the front entrance of the theatre, its beautiful façade and a big sign: Chev Community Theatre Presents: Home is Where the Heart Is. A crowd is gathered on the red carpet. The ethos and philosophy of the organisation, "No Jew gets left behind", is embossed on the red carpet.

Backstage, the director has assembled the cast in the Culture, Purpose and Leadership room. We see a reference to the Culture Print ("The Chev is a place where I, as an employee… ") and the purpose articulated in a speech bubble ("I finally get why we are here – to make our audience feel happy and safe"). The reference to how personal purpose connects to organisational purpose is seen via the lipstick on the mirror ("Why am I here?"). The philosophy of focusing on strengths is captured by the cast member in a Superman suit saying, "What's your superpower?"

On stage, we see the cast taking a bow. The songs playing represent the aspirational culture and are adapted from the Culture Print.

In the foyer we see the cast members signing autographs and receiving acknowledgement. They are wearing Chev T-shirts and thinking, "I am proud to be part of this family. I can't believe I get to come back and do this again."

The Chev Visual Map Discussion Manual

The Visual Map is a powerful tool. However, when used as a catalyst for leader-facilitated team conversations (guided by the manual), the true magic of the process is unleashed.

This manual was created as a guide for leaders to take their team through the content of the map. Carefully designed, it used generative questions around every aspect of the Visual Map – to stimulate positive conversations worth having. Story sharing was encouraged.

In addition to high levels of retention and memorability, the conversation around the visual map facilitated ownership and engagement. It revealed the compelling vision and purpose of the organisation, and as importantly, catalysed the emotional connection, the WIIFM for each employee.

Results

"Our Visual Map embodies such a deep, insightful understanding of our business. It is us! The launch was really incredible! SO well received and the teams really engaged with it. They are so excited to share it further with their teams." – Saul Thomson, CEO, shortly after the launch.

Quotes from the Chev employees:

"We were constantly looking for and seeing new things. This was unique, enticing and a lot of fun. I have never seen anything like this – I will never forget it."

"So mind-blowing! So exciting and so interactive! I'm so enthusiastic about this. It has motivated me to do even more for the Chev… I would work here for nothing!"

Two years after the launch, the world was upended by the Covid-19 pandemic. Upon checking in with Saul Thomson, the CEO, on how things were going I received the following response: “It really helps having a strong culture and united team at this unbelievably testing time.”

And a few months later: “One day we will do a case study of how this process enabled us to establish our shared culture and purpose and literally resulted in us being able to save lives during this pandemic.”

Appreciation

"Do not conform any longer to the patterns of this world, but be transformed by the renewing of your mind..." *Romans 12 v 2*

This is one of my favourite scriptures and I love its inherent challenge to "think differently". I am so grateful for God's grace, and for the blessing of being surrounded by incredible people who through many conversations, over many years, have sparked my thinking, renewed my mind and refreshed my soul.

Thank you to my family, friends, colleagues and clients, who have taken the time share their thoughts, insights and stories with me.

Thank you Wilhelm and Cia from Knowledge Resources, for your support, encouragement and expertise.

Thank you Mark and Shawn from Anecdote, our partners and friends, for developing and sharing the most amazing material – and for your inspiring passion to change the world.

Thank you Adam for always knowing exactly what I see in my mind's eye and for your incredible talent in visualising it.

Thank you Juanita, for your friendship and support, your eagle eye and your strengths-focused, just-do-it spirit.

Thank you Sandi, for being both a creative genius and a problem-solving ninja – with a delicious giggle that always makes my day.

Thank you Lis, my fellow THINKspirationist and precious friend, not only for your passion for this work, your wise insights, tenacious attention to detail and incredible patience, but for making work fun. Your sparkle makes every day a joy!

Thank you Mom and Robs for your love, support and prayers, and for teaching me that anything is possible, and that everything will always be ok in the end.

Most of all thank you to my two precious boys, Bernard and Zack. Bernard, not only did you inspire, encourage (and yes also nag) me every step of the way, you made this book yours along the many kilometres that we walked and talked: through every chapter, every concept and every edit. You inspire me every day - everything I have learned about leadership is because I have seen you do it first. My Zack (Kini), thank you for always reminding me that I have a "book to write" and thank you for being the living embodiment of so many of these principles (you still have to read the book though!). You give me hope for a better world every time you open your mouth!

References

- Apple. 1997. Here's to the crazy ones. Online video. YouTube. Available at: https://www.youtube.com/watch?v=tjgtLSHhTPg&ab_channel=vintagemacmuseum (Accessed on 30 November 2021).
- Brown, B. 2015a. Daring Greatly. New York: Avery.
- Brown, B. 2015b. Rising Strong. New York: Random House.
- Brown, B. 2018. Dare to Lead: Brave work. Tough conversations. Whole hearts. New York: Random House.
- Buckingham, M. & Goodall, A. 2019. Nine Lies About Work: A Freethinking Leader's Guide to the Real World. Boston: Harvard Business Review Press.
- Callahan, S. 2013. How to spot an oral story. Available at: https://www.anecdote.com/2013/10/spot-oral-story/ (Accessed on 30 November 2021).
- Callahan, S. 2015. The link between memory and stories. Available at: https://www.anecdote.com/2015/01/link-between-memory-and-stories/ (Accessed on 2 December 2021).
- Callahan, S. 2016. Putting stories to work: Mastering Business Storytelling. Melbourne, Australia: Pepperberg Press.
- Collis, D. J. & Rukstad. M.G. 2008. Can you say what your strategy is? Harvard Business Review. Available at: https://hbr.org/2008/04/can-you-say-what-your-strategy-is (Accessed on 25 November 2021).
- Covey, S. 2007. The business case for trust. ChiefExecutive. Available at: https://chiefexecutive.net/the-business-case-for-trust/ (Accessed on 25 November 2021).
- De Saint-Exupéry, A. 1968. Citadelle. Paris: Le livre de poche.
- Dourado, P. 2007. The 60 second leader. Hoboken, New Jersey: Wiley & Sons Inc.

- Dunbar, P. 2021. Upgrade your skills take risks focus on yourself. Red Magazine, 44-46.
- Dunbar, R. 2004. Gossip in Evolutionary Perspective. Review of General Psychology. 8(2), 100-110.
- Gallo, C. 2018. Jeff Bezos banned PowerPoint in Meetings. Available at: https://www.inc.com/carmine-gallo/jeff-bezos-bans-powerpoint-in-meetings-his-replacement-is-brilliant.html (Accessed on 24 November 2021).
- Gallup CliftonStrengths, (n.d.). An introduction to the Futuristic® CliftonStrengths Theme. Available at: https://www.gallup.com/cliftonstrengths/en/252248/futuristic-theme.aspx (Accessed on 28 November 2021).
- Gallup Inc. 2017. State of the American Workplace. Available at: https://www.gallup.com/workplace/238085/state-american-workplace-report-2017.aspx (Accessed on 30 November 2021).
- Goldman, J, 2013. Animating Anthromorphism: Giving minds to geometric shapes [Video]. Scientific American. Available at: https://blogs.scientificamerican.com/thoughtful-animal/animating-anthropomorphism-giving-minds-to-geometric-shapes-video/ (Accessed on 30 November 2021).
- Harter, J.K., Schmidt, F.L., Agrawal, S., Blue, A., Plowman, S.K., Josh, P., Asplund, J. 2020. The Relationship between engagement at work and Organizational Outcomes: 2020 Q12 Meta-Analysis: 10th Edition. (2020). Washington D.C. Gallup, Inc. Available at: https://www.gallup.com/workplace/321725/gallup-q12-meta-analysis-report.aspx (Accessed 23 November 2021).
- Haudan, J, 2018. Dialogue at Work is the oxygen of change!. Available at: https://www.rootinc.com/dialogue-at-work-is-the-oxygen-of-engagement-and-change/dialogue-at-work-is-the-oxygen-of-engagement-and-change/ (Accessed on 25 November 2021).

- Haudan, J. 2008. The Art of Engagement. New York: McGraw-Hill Education.
- Independent. 2018. Work is one of the first things that crosses Briton's minds as they wake up in the morning, study claims. Available at: https://www.independent.co.uk/news/uk/home-news/work-mind-morning-wake-up-study-thinking-a8360406.html (Accessed on 29 November 2021).
- Insel, T.R., Collins, P.Y., & Hyman, S.E. 2015. Darkness Invisible: The Hidden Global Costs of Mental Illness. Foreign Affairs, 94(1), 127–135. Available at: http://www.jstor.org/stable/24483225. (Accessed on 25 November 2021).
- Jarrett, J. 2019. Why meeting another's gaze is so powerful. BBC Future. Available at: https://www.bbc.com/future/article/20190108-why-meeting-anothers-gaze-is-so-powerful (Accessed on 30 November 2021).
- Jobs, S. 2011. CNET News: Steve Jobs introduces iCloud. Available at https://www.youtube.com/watch?v=O_C1TZIT-qQ&ab_channel=CNET. (Accessed on 15 Feb 2022).
- Kaplan, R.S., & Norton, D.P. 2005. The office of strategy management. Harvard business review, 83(10), 72–157.
- Keller, T & Keller, K. 2011. The Meaning of Marriage. New York: Dutton.
- Keltner, D. 2017. The Power Paradox – how we gain and lose influence. London: Penguin Books.
- Kennedy, J.F. 1962. John F. Kennedy Moon Speech – Rice Stadium. Available at: https://er.jsc.nasa.gov/seh/ricetalk.htm (Accessed on 30 November 2021).
- Kennedy, J.F. 1961. President Kennedy's Man on the Moon Speech. Online video. YouTube. Available at: https://www.youtube.com/watch?v=GhgVZLrxiu0&ab_channel=BritishMovietone (Accessed on 30 November 2021).

- King, M.L. 1963. Martin Luther King, Jr.: I have a Dream Speech. Available at: https://kr.usembassy.gov/education-culture/infopedia-usa/living-documents-american-history-democracy/martin-luther-king-jr-dream-speech-1963/ (Accessed on 30 November 2021).
- Kline, N. 2015. Time to Think: Listening to ignite the Human Mind. London: Cassell.
- Kotter, J.P., & Heskett, J.L. 2011. Corporate Culture and Performance. New York: Free Press.
- Lee, H. 1988. To Kill a Mockingbird. New York: Grand Central Publishing.
- Marquet, L.D. 2020. Leadership is Language: The hidden power of what you say – and what you don't. London: Portfolio.
- Murphy, K. 2020. You're not Listening: What you're missing and why it matters. New York: Celadon Books.
- Ngozi, A.C. 2009. The danger of a single story. Available at: https://www.ted.com/talks/chimamanda_ngozi_adichie_the_danger_of_a_single_story/transcript?language=en (Accessed on 30 November 2021).
- Olsen, E. 2006. Do you Employees Understand Your Strategy? On Strategy. Available at: https://onstrategyhq.com/resources/do-your-employees-understand-your-strategy/ (Accessed on 25 November 2021).
- Pollack, J. 2015. Shortcut: How Analogies reveal connections, spark innovation, and sell our greatest ideas. New York: Avery.
- Rigoni, B. & Asplund, J. 2017. Strengths-Based Cultures attract top talent. Gallup Workplace. Available at: https://www.gallup.com/workplace/236270/strengths-based-cultures-attract-top-talent.aspx (Accessed on 25 November 2021).

- Roosevelt, T. 1910. Address at the Sorbonne in Paris, France: "Citizenship in a Republic". Available at: http://www.worldfuturefund.org/Documents/maninarena.htm (Accessed on 25 November 2021).
- Sadowsky, J. 2019. Why stories form our native language. Available at: http://www.johnsadowsky.com/why-stories-form-our-native-language/ (Accessed on 30 November 2021).
- Schenk, M., & Bishop, K. 2011. Making strategies stick – tackling anti-stories. Anecdote. Available at: https://www.anecdote.com/pdfs/papers/Anecdote_Tackling_Anti-stories.pdf (Accessed on 30 November 2021).
- Seuss, T. 1959. Happy Birthday to You! New York: Random House.
- Shift Learning. 2014. Studies confirm the power of visuals to engage your audience in eLearning. Available at: https://www.shiftelearning.com/blog/bid/350326/studies-confirm-the-power-of-visuals-in-elearning (Accessed on 1 December 2021).
- Sill, M. 2021. What are Sunday scaries? And how can we beat them? Available at: https://www.linkedin.com/pulse/what-sunday-scaries-how-can-we-beat-them-mike-sill/ (Accessed 23 November 2021.
- Sinek, S. 2017. Dealing with Smartphone disrespect. Available at: https://www.youtube.com/watch?v=HTGRMWhclgM&ab_channel=100%25Entertainment (Accessed 7 January 2022).
- Soffel, J. 2016. Ten 21st-century skills every student needs. World Econonomic Forum Industry Agenda. Available at: https://www.weforum.org/agenda/2016/03/21st-century-skills-future-jobs-students/ (Accessed on 25 November 2021).
- Stavros, J., Cooperrider, D., & Kelley, L. 2003. 'Strategic inquiry with appreciative intent: Inspiration to SOAR!.' AI Practitioner: International Journal of Appreciative Inquiry, 5(4), 10-17.

- Sull, D., Homkes, R., & Sull. 2015. 'Why Strategy Execution Unravels-and What to Do About It.' Harvard Business Review, 93(3), 58-66.
- Swanepoel, T. 2016. The Leadership Riptide and how to Escape. Johannesburg: BizNews Online Services (Pty) Ltd.
- Terkel, S. 1997. Working: People Talk about What They Do All Day and How They Feel about What They Do. New York: New Press.
- The illusions index, (n.d.). Young Woman or Old Woman. Available at: https://www.illusionsindex.org/i/young-woman-or-old-woman (Accessed on 26 November 2021).
- Thoreau, H.D. 1998. Civil Disobedience: Solitude and Life without Principle. New York: Prometheus.

Endnotes

1 *Harter, Schmidt, Agrawal et al., 2020*
2 *Terkel, 1997*
3 *Sill, 2021*
4 *Gallup Press, 2017*
5 *Independent, 2018*
6 *Insel, Collins & Hyman, 2015*
7 *Gallup Press, 2017*
8 *Harter, Schmidt, Agrawal et al., 2020*
9 *Kotter & Heskett, 2011*
10 *Buckingham & Goodall, 2019*
11 *Buckingham & Goodall, 2019*
12 *Gallo, 2018*
13 *Kaplan & Norton, 2005*
14 *Olsen, 2006*
15 *Sull, Homkes & Sull, 2015*
16 *Haudan, 2018 Apple, 1997*
17 *Collis & Rukstad, 2008*
18 *Apple, 1997*
19 *John F Kennedy, 1961*
20 *Keltner, 2017*
21 *Brown, 2015a*
22 *Buckingham & Goodall, 2019*
23 *Seuss, 1959*
24 *Swanepoel, 2016*
25 *Swanepoel, 2016*
26 *Covey, 2007*
27 *Rigoni & Asplund, 2017*
28 *Mintzberg, as cited in Dourado, 2007: 48*
29 *Roosevelt, 1910*
30 *Buckingham & Goodall, 2019*
31 *Brown, 2015a*
32 *Keller & Keller, 2011*
33 *Soffel, 2016*
34 *Brown, 2018: 43*
35 *The Illusions index, n.d.*
36 *The Illusions index, n.d.*
37 *Thoreau, 1863*
38 *Murphy, 2020*
39 *Kline, 2015*
40 *Sinek, 2017*
41 *Jarret, 2019*
42 *Callahan, 2015*
43 *Dunbar, 2004*
44 *Sadowsky, 2019*
45 *Goldman, 2013*
46 *Brown, 2015*
47 *Callahan, 2013*
48 *Callahan, 2016*
49 *De St Exupery, 1968*
50 *Gallup CliftonStrengths, n.d.*
51 *Stavros, Cooperrider & Kelley, 2003*
52 *Ngozi Adichie, 2009*
53 *Lee, 1988*
54 *Schenk & Bishop, 2011*
55 *Jobs, 2011.*
56 *Callahan, 2016*
57 *Kaplan & Norton, 2005*
58 *Gallup Press, 2017*
59 *Gallup Inc, 2017*

60 *King, 1963*
61 *Kennedy, 1962*
62 *Apple, 1997*
63 *Pollack, 2015*
64 *Callahan, 2015*
65 *Haudan, 2008: 87*
66 *Pollack, 2015*
67 *Adapted from Zhang, as cited in Haudan, 2008.*
68 *Haudan, 2008*
69 *Pollack, 2015*
70 *Haudan, 2008*
71 *Marquet, 2020*
72 *Marquet, 2020*
73 *Dunbar, 2021: 45*

www.ingramcontent.com/pod-product-compliance
Lightning Source LLC
Chambersburg PA
CBHW061212220326
41599CB00025B/4614